# WIMBLED

## *Ladies' Singles Champions*

## 1884–2004

Maud Watson, the first champion; May Sutton, the first overseas champion; Suzanne Lenglen, undefeated at Wimbledon; Martina Navratilova, nine singles titles.

# WIMBLEDON
## *Ladies' Singles Champions*
### 1884–2004

John Barrett and Alan Little

Published in 2005 by
Wimbledon Lawn Tennis Museum
All England Lawn Tennis Club
Church Road, Wimbledon
London, SW19 5AE

A CIP catalogue record for this book
is available from the British Library

ISBN 0 906741 39 4

Designed by Roger Walker
Typeset in Bembo and Optima

Printed and bound in Great Britain by
L&S Printing Company Limited,
Worthing, West Sussex

# Contents

# Preface

This second edition of *Wimbledon – The Ladies Singles Champions* follows the same pattern as the original edition, published in 1984. A brief biographical sketch of each champion is followed by a complete record of their Wimbledon performances, together with outstanding career performances and personal details.

The original sketches were written by the late Lance Tingay, for so many years the lawn tennis correspondent of the *Daily Telegraph*. These have been retained for the most part with amendments and additions where necessary. The more recent biographies, from Martina Navratilova onwards, have been written by John Barrett, BBC Television's senior tennis commentator and the tennis correspondent of the *Financial Times*.

Alan Little, Honorary Librarian of the Wimbledon Lawn Tennis Museum, assembled the statistical information for the original edition, itself a monumental undertaking. For this second addition he has once again trawled the archives to produce the required facts.

It should be noted that all information up to the end of 2004 has been included.

June 2005

Billie Jean King, twenty Wimbledon titles.

# The Ladies' Singles Champions

Seven years after the first Gentlemen's Singles Championship, the ladies had their moment on Wednesday, 16th July 1884 when 13 players, one of whom withdrew, competed for the new Ladies' Singles Championship.

Between 1884 and 2004 there were 42 winners of the Ladies' Singles. They range from the virtually unknown Lena Rice, from Tipperary, who won from an entry of four in 1890, when the event had slipped to its nadir of fortune, to Martina Navratilova, who won the singles an unprecedented nine times between 1978 and 1990.

All were Queens of Wimbledon and the game is proud of them. Throughout the years the ladies have contributed charm and colour, excitement and drama and it is inconceivable that the meeting could fall back to being the all male preserve it was in its cradle years.

If all were queens, some merit a higher title as Empresses. No player, man or woman, did more to popularise the meeting than the dynamic, imperious and invincible Suzanne Lenglen, who reigned from 1919 to 1925. Helen Wills was equally dominant in the 1930s, as was Martina Navratilova in the 1980s.

For more than two decades the domesticity of Wimbledon was unimpaired. It was 1905 before a winner came from overseas – the incursion of Lena Rice in 1890 can hardly be counted as such – when May Sutton of California became the first successful invader. Since 1919 there have been only five British winners.

The age range of the singles champions is wide. Lottie Dod, the wonderful all-rounder from Cheshire, was 15 years 285 days old when she won on 6th July 1887. Charlotte Sterry was 37 years 282 days when she won for the fifth time on 30th June 1908.

Lottie Dod won five times and was never beaten though there were never more than nine entrants during her winning years. There were other invincibles. Suzanne Lenglen, six times singles champion, Pauline Betz, who played but once, and Maureen Connolly with three victories.

The longest gap between singles success was by that wonderful stalwart of the early years, Blanche Bingley-Hillyard. Her first singles title was in 1886, her sixth in 1900, an interval of 14 years. Charlotte Sterry first won in 1895 so her interval was but a year less at 13. The only other champions to have a gap of more than a decade have been Martina Navratilova, 1978–1990, Dorothea Chambers, 1903–1914 and Helen Wills Moody, 1927–1938.

As to the gap between competing in the singles, no one matches the record of Martina Navratilova, who first played in 1973 and for the 23rd time in 2004, 31 years later. Blanche Hillyard played at the inaugural event in 1884 and for the 24th time no less than 29 years later in 1913. Charlotte Sterry had a gap of 26 years between her first singles challenge in 1893 and her last in 1919 when it was her 18th appearance.

The most recent British Queen, Virginia Wade, played in the singles for 24 consecutive years, 1962–1985. In 1983, the ubiquitous Billie Jean King, with 20 titles, six singles, ten doubles and four mixed behind her, competed in the singles 22 years after her first challenge in 1961.

Six of the champions won at the first attempt – Maud Watson, Lottie Dod, May Sutton, Suzanne Lenglen, Pauline Betz and Maureen Connolly.

# Maud Watson

## 1884, 1885

## *The Trail Blazer*

Maud Watson is assured of lawn tennis immortality. In 1884 she won the inaugural Ladies' Championship. She was the leader. She blazed the trail. All other champions can only be her followers.

Maud was 19 years old when on Saturday July 19th 1884 she became the winner of the newly instituted Ladies' Singles Championship. Like the new Gentlemen's Doubles event it was staged after the completion of the Gentlemen's Singles. It was not the pioneer event of its kind for the All England Lawn Tennis Club had dragged its feet rather in encouraging the women into competitive action. The Irish had been more progressive five years earlier.

Two years after that, 1881, Maud, then only 16, had played at Edgbaston, virtually a home tournament, and won the singles. By that time she was living in her family home in Berkswell, near Coventry, where her father, the Reverend Henry William Watson was rector. He was a mathematician of some note and had formerly taught at Harrow School.

At the All England Lawn Tennis Club by the side of the railway in Worple Road, Maud Watson was the winner from an entry of 13. She lost two sets, the first in the semi-final against Blanche Bingley, a player who was later to eclipse all rivals. In the final she lost the opening set also – to Miss Watson.

That is how the early records had it. Miss Maud Watson beat Miss Watson 6–8 6–3 6–3. Nothing could have been more precise and correct according to the custom of the time. Since Maud Watson was the younger sister she was called Miss Maud Watson. Her elder sister was allowed to dispense with her Christian name.

Miss Watson was Miss Lilian Watson, Maud's elder sister by some seven years. The inaugural final at Wimbledon was a family affair. The triumphant Maud had youth and dash and flair. Moreover she could volley and served overhead.

In 1885 Maud, playing through, won for the second time, not losing a set and beat Miss Bingley in the final. The next year a challenge trophy was presented and so the lady champion had, like the man, the privilege of 'standing out' until the Challenge Round. The ubiquitous Blanche Bingley came through as challenger and beat Maud in two sets. It was Maud's last match at Wimbledon and she gave up competition after 1888.

The pioneering champion went on living in Berkswell until 1932 and was awarded an M.B.E. for her nursing work in World War I. She was at the Wimbledon Jubilee celebrations in 1926 and Helen Wills Moody has recounted how in the 1930s she was approached by Maud in her London hotel and wished good luck in her coming final.

**Wimbledon Singles Record:**
1884, won 4 matches, champion (sets 8–2; games 58–33).
1885, won 3 matches, champion (sets 6–0: games 37–9).
1886, won 0 matches, lost Blanche Bingley, Challenge Round.

**Matches:** 7–1; sets 14–4; games 101–54.

**Longest Match:** Final, 1884, beat Lilian Watson 6–8 6–3 6–3 – a total of 32 games.

**Age on first winning singles:** 19 years 284 days

**Age on last winning singles:** 20 years 281 days

**Career Achievements:**
*The Championships, Wimbledon:* singles 1884, 1885.
*Irish Championships:* singles 1884, 1885, doubles 1885.
*Welsh Championships:* singles 1887.

**Full name:** Maud Edith Eleanor Watson
**Born:** 9th October, 1864, Harrow, Middlesex, England.
**Died:** 5th June, 1946, Charmouth, Dorset, England, aged 81.

# Blanche Bingley/Hillyard

## 1886, 1889, 1894, 1897, 1899, 1900

### *The Tireless Enthusiast*

Blanche Bingley, then a 20 year old from Greenford in Middlesex, competed in the inaugural Ladies' Singles at Wimbledon in 1884. She won two matches before losing to the first champion, Maud Watson in the semi-finals. In 1912, when she was 48 and had been married for a quarter of a century to George Hillyard and had six times won the title, she competed for the 23rd time and again reached the semi-finals where she lost to the champion Ethel Larcombe.

She also competed in 1913, her 24th challenge. She was 49 and lost in the opening round. What an indefatigable player she was!

Her quarter-final win in 1912 brought together what were perhaps the two most tireless competitors of all times, for she beat Elizabeth Ryan, the Californian who was destined to go on and win 19 Wimbledon titles, though never the singles. Miss Ryan probably played more lawn tennis than anyone up to 1934 when she became a professional. In 1924 she played in 33 tournaments and won all three events in 17 of them.

Blanche Hillyard, as she became in 1887, would probably have played in as many had she not flourished at a time when there were fewer events to engage her enthusiasm. But like Miss Ryan she was on the 'circuit' week after week.

It was appropriate, then, that in 1912 Blanche won her last singles at Wimbledon by beating the Californian 3–6 8–6 6–3. It was Miss Ryan's first defeat.

Her husband, George, was equally keen and was Secretary of the All England Lawn Tennis Club from 1907 to 1924. Their house parties at Thorpe-Satchville in Leicestershire were, in the halcyon decades before and after the turn of the century, notable lawn tennis events in themselves.

Her contemporaries held Blanche in awe and her sporting nature, despite her frown when concentrating, was a by-word. She was, wrote Harry Scrivener, "an alert, confident and plucky player".

Her rival Charlotte Sterry wrote that if Blanche Hillyard headed the list of the most victoriuos players she "is one of the most sporting of them. Certainly no keener player ever stepped on a tennis court. It does not matter if her adversary happens to be a third-class player, to whom she could owe 40 and give 30; she is always just as nice as if she were her equal".

At a time when many women, perhaps the majority, still served underarm, she served overarm.

Blanche is unique among women in being a Wimbledon competitor 30 years after her debut. In her valedictory singles Ethel Hannam of Somerset beat her 4–6 6–2 6–0.

There was a span of 14 years between her first and last championships, 1886 and 1900 and in winning at the age of 36 she stands as the second oldest winner of the ladies' singles. In 1908 Mrs. Sterry was a year older.

Her longest life as champion was in the South of England meeting on the grass at Eastbourne, for years an event of the highest prestige. Blanche won the singles first in 1885 and for the 11th time in 1905, a span of 20 years.

### Wimbledon Singles Record:

1884, won 2 matches, lost Maud Watson, semi-final.

1885, won 2 matches, lost Maud Watson, final.

1886, won 4 matches, champion (sets 8–0; games 50–20)

1887, won 0 matches, lost Lottie Dod, Challenge Round.

1888, won 2 matches, lost Lottie Dod, Challenge Round.

1889, won 3 matches, champion (sets 6–1; games 44–26).

1890, did not play.

1891, won 2 matches, lost Lottie Dod, All-Comers' final.

1892, won 3 matches, lost Lottie Dod, Challenge Round.

1893, won 2 matches, lost Lottie Dod, Challenge Round.

1894, won 3 matches, champion (sets 6–0; games 36–5).

1895, did not play.

1896, did not play.

1897, won 3 matches, champion (sets 6–1; games 43–22).

1898, did not play.

1899, won 5 matches, champion (sets 10–2; games 72–43).
1900, won 1 match, champion (sets 2–1; games 16–14).
1901, won 0 matches, lost Charlotte Sterry, Challenge Round.
1902, won 0 matches, lost Hilda Lane, 2nd round.
1903, did not play.
1904, won 2 matches, lost Winifred Longhurst, 3rd round.
1905, won 4 matches, lost Constance Wilson, semi-final.
1906, won 3 matches, lost Beryl Tulloch, 2nd round.
1907, won 3 matches, lost Constance Wilson, semi-final.
1908, won 1 match, lost Beryl Tulloch 2nd, round.
1909, won 0 matches, lost Aurea Edgington, 2nd round.
1910, won 1 match, lost Winifred McNair, 3rd round.
1911, did not play.
1912, won 2 matches, lost Ethel Larcombe, semi-final.
1913, won 0 matches, lost Ethel Hannam, 2nd round.

**Matches:** 48–18; sets 103–46; games 770–544.

**Longest match:** semi-final, 1905, lost to Constance Wilson 5–7 11–9 2–6 – a total of 40 games.

**Age on first winning singles:** 22 years 256 days.

**Age on last winning singles:** 36 years 242 days.

**Career Achievements:**
*The Championships, Wimbledon:* singles 1886, 1889, 1894, 1897, 1899, 1900.
*German Championships:* singles 1897, 1900.
*Irish Championships:* singles 1888, 1894, 1897; mixed 1894, 1897.
*Welsh Championships:* singles 1888.

**Full name:** Blanche Bingley/Hillyard
**Born:** 3rd November, 1863,Greenford, Middlesex, England.
**Married:** George Hillyard on 13th July, 1887, Greenford, Middlesex, England.
**Died:** 6th August, 1946, Pulborough, Sussex, England, aged 82.

Miss B. Bingley.

# Lottie Dod

## 1887, 1888, 1891–1893

### Invincible All-Rounder

After the pioneer achievements of Maud Watson and the initial success of Blanche Bingley there came, in 1887, the most notable woman champion of the 19th century. Lottie Dod. She was the first of the invincibles. In five championships, 1887, 1888, 1891, 1892 and 1893 she was never beaten.

She had another distinction. She was the youngest champion – and of either sex, singles or doubles. She was 15 years 285 days old in 1887 when, wearing the comparitvely unrestricted short skirts permissible for a schoolgirl, she won for the first time. It was a record that would stand for more than a century. Not until Martina Hingis won the Ladies' Doubles with Helena Sukova in 1996 was there a younger champion.

Lottie was mobile and a good volleyer. None the less she served underarm. Indeed she wrote that the effort of learning an overhead service was not, for women, worth while. One must class her as the first of the women 'stars'. She had what today would be called charisma and her skill and charm has echoed down the years. In the 1930s there were many older enthusiasts who muttered that the immortal Lottie Dod was, despite Suzanne Lenglen and Helen Wills Moody, the greatest of them all.

Charlotte Dod was born at Lower Bebington, Cheshire, the youngest of four children of a wealthy cotton-broker. There were two courts, one hard and one grass, in her garden. She began lawn tennis at the age of nine and an elder brother gave her a sharp edge from the first. She played in her first tournament, the Northern Championships in Manchester, in 1883. She won first prize in the consolation doubles. She was 11.

In 1886, when 14, the precocious Lottie won the West of England title in Bath. She beat the then invincible Maud Watson in the final.

A year later she took Wimbledon in a canter. Only three matches were necessary and her total loss of games was only nine. Her Challenge Round victim was Miss Bingley. The same player, now Mrs. G.W. Hillyard, came through to challenge Lottie as the holder one year later. Lottie's concession was six games.

Bored with tennis, she did not return to Wimbledon until 1891. Then her three victories in the All-Comers' singles cost her only seven games and there was no holder to defend the Challenge Round, Lena Rice remaining in Ireland. She defended her title against the challenge of Mrs. Hillyard in 1892. The same player challenged her a year later and this was the only time Lottie was extended to three sets.

Having done all she could do in the lawn tennis she turned to golf. She played for England in many internationals. In 1904 she won the British Women's Championship at Troon.

At the same time hockey was her winter sport. She was twice capped for England, against Ireland in 1899 and 1900.

Archery was a pleasant sideline. Her brother William was rather good and he won the gold medal at the Olympic Games of 1908 in London. Lottie had to be content with a silver medal. She shot for England and was South of England Champion that year.

She excelled also in winter sports. At skating she passed both the men's and women's test at St. Moritz. She did the Cresta Run. She was also something of a mountaineer. She rowed. She also rode.

She had a contralto voice well above average quality and was a member of the London Oriana Madrigal Society. She was Honorary Secretary of that body for some time. She played the piano.

Was there ever such an awesome array of talent as that? In World War I she nursed. She died, unmarried, at the age of 88. At that time she was reputed to play a good hand of bridge.

## Wimbledon Singles Record

1887, won 3 matches, champion (sets 6–0; games 36–9).
1888, won 1 match champion (sets 2–0; games 12–6).
1891, won 3 matches champion (sets 6–0; games 36–7).
1892, won 1 match champion (sets 2–0; games 12–2).
1893, won 1 match champion (sets 2–1; games 18–13).

**Matches:** 9–0; sets 18–1; games 114–37.

**Longest match:** Challenge Round 1893, beat Blanche Hillyard 6–8 6–1 6–4 – a total of 31 games.

**Age on first winning singles:** 15 years 285 days.

**Age on last winning singles:** 21 years 297 days.

**Career Achievements:**
*The Championships, Wimbledon:* singles 1887, 1888, 1891, 1892, 1893.
*Irish Championships:* singles 1887; doubles 1892; mixed 1887.

**Full name:** Charlotte Dod
**Born:** 24th September, 1871, Bebington, Cheshire, England.
**Died:** 27th June, 1960, Sway, Hampshire, England, aged 88.

Miss L. Dod,
Winner of the Ladies Championship.

# Lena Rice

## 1890

## *Irish Anonymity*

Helena Bertha Grace Rice, to give the 1890 champion her full name, was born on June 21st 1866 at New Inn, County Tipperary and she died unmarried, on June 21st, her fortieth birthday, in the same village. Of no champion is less known about her origins. She blossomed for just two years and that at a time when Wimbledon's fortunes were at their lowest.

Her distinction in the saga of Wimbledon's heroines is that she qualifies as the least distinguished. Could she have been more Irish than that?

Lena competed in the Irish Championships at the Fitzwilliam Club, Dublin, in 1889 with another Irish player, Willoughby Hamilton. They won the mixed doubles. She came to Wimbledon, beat Miss M. Jacks 6–2 6–0 and was then beaten in the All Comers' final 4–6 8–6 6–4 by Blanche Hillyard after having three match points in the second set. The total entry in the event was six.

In 1890 the total entry was even less, four. Lena beat Mary Steedman 7–5 6–2 and then met Miss Jacks again in the All Comers' final. Since Mrs. Hillyard was not defending her title it was the championship match. Lena won 6–4 6–1. There must have been rejoicing in the Irish camp that year. Hamilton won the Gentlemen's singles title also.

Because of the death of her mother, Lena did not come back to defend in 1891 and retired from the game. The event livened then for it marked the return of the invincible Lottie Dod.

**Wimbledon Singles Record:**
1889, won 1 match, lost All Comers' final to Blanche Hillyard.
1890, won 2 matches, champion (sets 4–0; games 25–12).

**Matches:** 3–1; sets 7–2; games 53–32.

**Longest Match:** All Comers' final, 1889, lost to Blanche Hillyard 6–4 6–8 4–6 – at total of 34 games.

**Age on winning singles:** 24 years 14 days.

**Career Achievements:**
*The Championships, Wimbledon:* singles 1890.
*Irish Championships:* mixed 1889.

**Full name:** Helena Bertha Grace Rice
**Born:** 21st June, 1866, New Inn, Co. Tipperary, Ireland.
**Died:** 21st June, 1907, New Inn, Co. Tipperary, Ireland, aged 41.

# Charlotte Cooper/Sterry

1895, 1896, 1898, 1901, 1908

## The Enthusiast

Not least among the notable women pio-
neers was the persistent and enthusiastic
Charlotte Sterry. As Charlotte Cooper she
was 22 years old when she competed at
Wimbledon for the first time in 1893 when
she was one of eight challengers. In 1919
she competed for the 18th time, under her
married identity from 1901.

Her five singles successes, the first in
1895, the last in 1908, put her among the
immortals. Yet it seems it was for her a
matter of fact affair. There is a delightful
story about her while living with her parents in Surbiton. When competing at
Wimbledon she used to cycle there, with
her racket, as was the custom in those halcyon days of the bicycle, clipped to a
bracket on the front fork. One evening she
turned in at the front gate to find her father
clipping the hedge.

"Where have you been, dear?" he
asked.

"Oh, to Wimbledon of course, father" she replied.

"Ah, yes. You mentioned it, I remember. You were playing the final, weren't
you. Did you win?"

"Yes, as a matter of fact I did."

"I'm so glad," said her father.

In 1902 she was involved in the queerest Challenge Round of all time. She
defended her title against the challenge of Muriel Robb. They began in horrible
conditions and the match was stopped at one set all. Prior to its resumption the next
day it was decreed that the match should start all over again, with the upshot that
Miss Robb, having stood 4–6 13–11, won by 7–5 6–1. No other ladies' final was
extended over 53 games.

Charlotte's greatest rival was the tireless Blanche Hillyard. She successfully challenged her in 1901 to reverse their normal form. Her win in 1908 was her fifth and she was 37 years 282 days old. She stands as the most senior champion. She was 43 when she last played in 1919.

Her daughter was Gwen Sterry, British Wightman Cup player in 1927. Her son was Rex Sterry, for many years vice-chairman of the All England Lawn Tennis Club.

In 1961 she flew from Edinburgh to attend the 75th anniversary celebrations. She was unaccompanied. She was in her 91st year. She died at 96.

**Wimbledon Singles Record:**

1893, won 1 match, lost Blanche Hillyard, semi-final.

1894, won 1 match, lost Edith Austin, semi-final.

1895, won 3 matches, champion (sets 6–2; games 54–38).

1896, won 1 match, champion (sets 2–0; games 12–5).

1897, won 0 matches, lost Blanche Hillyard, Challenge round.

1898, won 4 matches champion (sets 8–1; games 52–32).

1899, won 0 matches, lost Blanche Hillyard, Challenge round.

1900, won 4 matches, lost Blanche Hillyard, Challenge round.

1901, won 6 matches, champion (sets 12–0; games 72–25).

1902, won 0 matches, lost Muriel Robb, Challenge round.

1903, did not compete.

1904, won 4 matches, lost Dorothea Douglass, Challenge round.

1905, did not compete.

1906, won 5 matches, lost Dorothea Douglass, All-Comers' final.

1907, won 0 matches, lost Gladys Eastlake Smith, 1st round.

1908, won 5 matches, champion (sets 10–0; games 61–31).

1909–1911, did not compete.

1912, won 4 matches, lost Ethel Larcombe, All-Comers' final.

1913, won 2 matches, lost Winifred McNair, semi-final.
1914, won 2 matches, lost Ethel Larcombe, 3rd round.
1919, won 1 match, lost Aurea Edgington, 3rd round.

**Matches:** 43–13; sets 92–36; games 719–524.

**Longest Match:** Challenge round 1902, lost (6–4 11–13) 5–7 1–6 to Muriel Robb with the
match restarted – a total of 53 games.
Third round 1919 lost to Aurea Edgington 6–8 11–9 3–6 – a total of 43 games.

**Age on first winning singles:** 24 years 296 days.

**Age on last winning singles:** 37 years 282 days.

**Career Achievements:**
*The Championships, Wimbledon:* singles 1895, 1896, 1898, 1901, 1908.
*Irish Championships:* singles 1895, 1898; mixed 1895, 1896, 1899, 1900.
*Scottish Championships:* singles 1899.
*Olympic Games:* singles, 1900 gold; mixed, 1900 gold

**Full name:** Charlotte Reinagle Cooper/Sterry
**Born:** 22nd September, 1870, Ealing, Middlesex, England.
**Married:** Alfred Sterry on 12th January, 1901, Surbiton, Surrey, England.
**Died:** 10th October, 1966, Helensburgh, Scotland, aged 96.

# Muriel Robb

## 1902

### *The Four Sets Champion*

The career of Muriel Evelyn Robb, who came from Newcastle, was brief, covering the turn of the century when Blanche Hillyard and Charlotte Sterry headed the British game. She was four months younger than the even more formidable Dorothea Douglass who, as Mrs. Chambers from 1907, began her long and successful stint as champion when Muriel gave up the challenge.

In the first three of her four Wimbledons Muriel was a quarter-finalist. In 1899 she lost to Mrs. Ruth Durlacher. The more formidable Mrs. Sterry accounted for her in 1900 and 1901. In that latter year it was very formidable indeed, Mrs. Sterry beating her 6–0 6–0.

Then followed Muriel's unique year of glory, 1902. Notably she beat Dorothea Douglass in the semi-finals. And a hard won victory it was, by an exhausting 6–4 2–6 9–7. It signposted Muriel's unexpected triumph.

Having beaten Agnes Morton to win the All Comers' singles Muriel challenged Mrs. Sterry for the title on Tuesday 1st July. It was the English summer at its worst. In dreadful weather the two struggled gamely but unhappily. After losing the first set 4–6 Muriel hung on and eventually won the second set 13–11. It was a miserable performance for all. The committee decreed that it should never have taken place at all, that the final should be started anew the next day.

So it was that in a fresh start Muriel made herself the champion. She won 7–5 6–1. In playing standards the match does not rank as one of the greater climaxes. The abandoned set if 13–11 was the longest in the ladies' final until Margaret Court and Billie Jean King wrestled to their noble 14–12 affair in 1970. As for the grand total of 53 games taken up by Muriel and Mrs. Sterry, the number has not been surpassed.

Muriel did not defend her strangely won title. She died less than five years later, at the age of 28.

**Wimbledon Singles Record:**
1899, won 1 match, lost Ruth Durlacher, quarter-final.
1900, won 1 match, lost Charlotte Cooper, quarter-final.
1901, won 2 matches, lost Charlotte Sterry, quarter-final.
1902, won 5 matches, champion (sets 11–3; games 88–65).

**Matches:** 9–3; sets 20–12; games 170–158.

**Longest Match:** Challenge round 1902, beat Charlotte Sterry (4–6 13–11) 7–5 6–1 – a total
of 53 games.
First round, 1901 she beat Ruth Winch 7–9 6–4 6–4 – a total of 36 games.

**Age on winning singles:** 24 years 41 days.

**Career Achievements:**
*The Championships,*
*Wimbledon:* singles 1902.
*Irish Championships:* singles
1901.
*Scottish Championships:* singles
1901.
*Welsh Championships:* singles
1899.

**Full name:** Muriel Evelyn Robb
**Born:** 13th May, 1878,
Newcastle,
Northumberland, England.
**Died:** 12th February, 1907,
Newcastle,
Northumberland, England,
aged 28.

# Dorothea Douglass/Chambers

## 1903, 1904, 1906, 1910, 1911, 1913, 1914

### *The pre-1914 Invincible*

A new era in lawn tennis came with the end of the first world war and, in the women's game, with domination from 1919 of the incomparable Suzanne Lenglen. The turning point was marked by one of the most dramatic contests in history, when in the Challenge Round at Wimbledon Suzanne beat the old champion 10–8 4–6 9–7. Dorothea Chambers had two match points before she surrendered and had she kept her title it would have been for the eighth time. She was 40 years old.

A young invincible replaced an old invincible. When in 1914 Dorothea thrust back the challenge of Ethel Larcombe 7–5 6–4 it meant that she had not conceded a set since losing to Charlotte Sterry in 1908.

In two years she had not played – for she was married and needed time off to produce her family – but she had twice played through the singles to win and twice kept her title in the challenge round. It was a four year's invincibility in which she won 13 matches and did not lose a set.

Indeed in 1911 she achieved the most one sided success in the history of lawn tennis. She became Wimbledon champion without losing a game! That was the year when Dora Boothby was beaten 6–0 6–0.

The reputation of Dorothea did not depend on such a freak result as that. Born in Ealing, Middlesex, the daughter of the Vicar of St. Matthews, Rev. Henry Douglass, she played at Wimbledon in 1900 when she was 19. She won for the first time in 1903. Her rivalry with the robust American challenger, May Sutton, endured three years. In 1905 Miss Sutton had the best of it. Dorothea took the crown back from her in 1906, conceded it again in 1907.

Like Miss Sutton her strength was her forehand, not so much in its pace but in its flexibility. Her short angled shot across the court was a notorious winner. Even so she was a relatively late developer. A chronic wrist injury was not completely mended until the end of the first decade of the century and until the outbreak of the war she was without a peer.

Of her seven Wimbledon singles, Dorothea won four by 'playing through'. She played for the title 11 times in all. She lost four. Two, 1905 and 1907, were to May Sutton. The other two, 1919 and 1920, were to Suzanne Lenglen.

Her achievement in 1920 in again getting to the Challenge Round (where she then won only three games from Suzanne) stressed her evergreen quality. She was then 41.

None the less she went on competing at Wimbledon, albeit only in the doubles. In 1925 and 1926 she was called to help Great Britain in the Wightman Cup. In 1925 she played in the number three singles position and beat Eleanor Goss 7–5 3–6 6–1 to help the British 4–3 success at Forest Hills. She also won her doubles. She was 46 years old. She lost her doubles when she was again the British captain at Wimbledon the following year.

Her last challenge in The Championships was in 1927 when she partnered the South African Billie Tapscott (who that year was the first woman to play at Wimbledon without stockings!) and came through one round. She was almost 49 years old.

She became a professional coach in 1928. Her other game was badminton, at which she was All England women's doubles champion in 1903 and mixed champion in 1904. She also played hockey for Middlesex.

**Wimbledon Singles Record:**
1900, won 0 matches, lost Louise Martin, 1st round.
1901, won 1 match, lost Charlotte Sterry, 2nd round.
1902, won 1 match, lost Muriel Robb, semi-final.
1903, won 3 matches, champion, (sets 6–1; games 40–20).
1904, won 1 match, champion, (sets 2–0; games 12–3).
1905, won 0 matches, lost May Sutton Challenge Round.
1906, won 6 matches, champion, (sets 12–0; games 75–32).
1907, won 0 matches, lost May Sutton, Challenge Round.
1908, won 2 matches, lost Charlotte Sterry, 3rd round.
1909, did not play.
1910, won 6 matches, champion, (sets 12–0; games 72–16).
1911, won 1 match, champion, (sets 2–0; games 12–0).
1912, did not play.
1913, won 5 matches, champion, (sets 10–0; games 60–19).
1914, won 1 match, champion, (sets 2–0; games 13–9).
1919, won 0 matches, lost Suzanne Lenglen, Challenge Round.
1920, won 5 matches, lost Suzanne Lenglen, Challenge Round.

**Matches:** 32–8; sets 66–19; games 481–263.

**Longest Match:** Challenge Round 1919, lost to Suzanne Lenglen 10–8 4–6 9–7 – a total of 44 games.

**Age on first winning singles:** 24 years 300 days.

**Age on last winning singles:** 35 years 305 days.

**Overall Record:**

| | Titles | Matches | | |
| --- | --- | --- | --- | --- |
| | | Played | Won | Lost |
| Singles | 7 | 40 | 32 | 8 |
| Doubles | 0 | 40 | 29 | 11 |
| Mixed | 0 | 35 | 24 | 11 |
| Total | 7 | 115 | 85 | 30 |

**Career Achievements:**
*The Championships, Wimbledon:* singles 1903, 1904, 1906, 1910, 1911, 1913, 1914.
*Olympic Games:* singles, 1908, gold.
*British Wightman Cup team:* 1925, 1926, winning 2 from 3 matches (singles 1–0; doubles 1–1).

**Full name:** Dorothea Katherine Douglass/Chambers
**Born:** 3rd September, 1878, Ealing, Middlesex, England.
**Married:** Robert Chambers on 6th April, 1907, Ealing, Middlesex, England.
**Died:** 7th January, 1960, Kensington, London, England, aged 81.

# May Sutton

## 1905, 1907

### The First Invader

May Sutton has a unique place in Wimbledon's history. She was not only the first American to win a title but she was also the first overseas challenger of any kind, man or woman to win.

She did so in 1905 at her first attempt. She was in fact only the second American woman to challenge. The first had been Marion Jones who had played without particular distinction in 1900.

May stands as a piquant figure, not least because, if American, she was undeniably British as well. She was born in Plymouth, Devon. Her father, a British naval captain, emigrated to California with his family. His was a noted lawn tennis family. Not only did May excel but so did her sisters, Violet, Florence and Ethel.

May came to England at the age of 18 and, having done well in earlier British tournaments, displayed her strong forehand with devastating effect at Wimbledon. In the Challenge Round she brought down Dorothea Douglass, later Mrs. Chambers, 6–3 6–4. She was a stocky, cheerful lass and was immediately popular.

A year later she yielded her title to the challenge of Miss Douglass. In 1907 she returned to win it back again. She achieved something of a *tour de force* when she returned to Wimbledon in 1929 at the age of 42. In the fourth round she beat Eileen Bennett, then the second ranking player in Great Britain.

Her skill and enthusiasm were long lasting. She played in the U.S. Wightman Cup in 1925. She was then 38 and was in the doubles with Mrs. Chambers, who was 46, on the other side. The British pair won that match.

Her daughter, Dodo, who had like enthusiasm, was Australian Champion in 1938 and also played in the Wightman Cup.

**Wimbledon Singles Record:**
1905, won 7 matches, champion, (sets 14–0; games 88–35).
1906, won 0 matches, lost Dorothea Douglass, Challenge Round.
1907, won 7 matches, champion, (sets 14–0; games 84–31).
1929, unseeded, won 2 matches, lost Joan Ridley, quarter-final.

**Matches:** 16–2; sets 32–6; games 218–119.

**Longest Match:** 4th round 1929, beat Eileen Bennett 3–6 6–4 6–4 – a total of 29 games.

**Age on first winning singles:** 18 years 286 days.

**Age on last winning singles:** 20 years 283 days.

**Career Achievements:**
*The Championships, Wimbledon:* singles 1905, 1907.
*U.S. Championships:* singles 1904; doubles 1904.
*U.S. Wightman Cup team:* 1925, winning 1 doubles.

**Full name:** May Godfray Sutton/Bundy
**Born:** 25th September, 1886, Plymouth, Devon, England.
**Married:** Thomas Bundy on 11th December, 1912, Los Angeles, California, U.S.A.
**Died:** 4th October, 1975, Santa Monica, California, U.S.A., aged 89.

# Dora Boothby

## 1909

### *The Whitewashed Champion*

Penelope Dora Harvey Boothby, who came from Finchley, won her only championship in 1909 when she was 27. It was a year when neither giant of that time, Charlotte Sterry and Dorothea Chambers, competed. The title match was the All Comers' final against Agnes Morton from Halstead in Essex, who later became Lady Stewart.

It was an arduous contest, Dora winning by 6–4 4–6 8–6. One critic wrote of it "There have been more scientific, more stroke-varied ladies' finals at Wimbledon but none in which the result hung so long in the balance or in which the combatants showed such hardihood and such resolution".

Mrs. Chambers resumed her challenge the next year and Dora relinquished her title to a score of 6–2 6–2. In the year after that, 1911, she participated in a title match that will stand out as long as Wimbledon records exist.

Her resolution in 1911 was sufficient to give Dora victory in the All Comers' singles without losing a set. She earned a place in the Challenge Round against Mrs. Chambers. It was her third title match in as many years. Mrs. Chambers was then 32 and possibly at her peak, even if her greatest final, that of 1919, lay some years in the future.

Dora probably had few illusions about her capacity to check the great champion. In the event the inevitable win was achieved not merely easily but shatteringly. There was never a title match like it before, nor one since. Mrs. Chambers beat Dora 6–0 6–0.

It did not deter Dora competing again in subsequent years, the last time in 1921. She was a noted badminton player and won the All England mixed title in 1909.

She was perhaps the only Ladies' Singles champion to have more fame in losing than in winning.

**Wimbledon Singles Record:**
1904, won 1 match, lost Winifred Longhurst, 2nd round.
1905, won 2 matches, lost Blanche Hillyard, quarter-final.
1906, won 0 matches, lost Charlotte Sterry, 1st round.
1907, won 0 matches, lost Toupee Lowther, 1st round.
1908, won 2 matches, lost Charlotte Sterry, quarter-final.
1909, won 5 matches, champion, (sets 10–1; games 63–35).
1910, won 0 matches, lost Dorothea Chambers, Challenge Round.
1911, won 5 matches, lost Dorothea Chambers, Challenge Round.
1912, won 1 match, lost Charlotte Sterry, 3rd round.
1913, won 1 match, lost Phyllis Satterthwaite, 2nd round.
1914, did not play.
1919, did not play.
1920, won 1 match, lost Molla Mallory, 2nd round.
1921, won 1 match, lost Molla Mallory, 3rd round.

**Matches:** 19–11; sets 39–26; games 314–282.

**Longest Match:** All Comers' Final 1909 beat Agnes Morton 6–4 4–6 8–6 – a total of 34 games.

**Age on winning singles:** 27 years 334 days.

**Career Achievements:**
*The Championships, Wimbledon:* singles 1909; doubles 1913.
*Olympic Games:* singles, 1908, silver

**Full name:** Penelope Dora Harvey Boothby/Geen
**Born:** 2nd August, 1881, Finchley, London, England.
**Married:** Arthur Geen on 14th April, 1914, London, England.
**Died:** 22nd February, 1970, Hammersmith, London, England, aged 88.

# Ethel Larcombe

## 1912

### The 'Lazy Champion'

Ethel Thomson, to give her maiden name, was a doctor's daughter from Islington, Middlesex. It is quite a striking fact that of all the British winners of the ladies' singles 1900 to 1914, all, Mrs. Chambers, Mrs. Sterry, Mrs. Hillyard, Dora Boothby, Ethel Larcombe, were from Middlesex and only Muriel Robb, from Northumberland, was not.

Ethel first competed at Wimbledon in 1902. She won her only championship ten years later having built a reputation as a fine doubles player. Her backhand down the line was said to be exceptional. She had a distinctive round arm smash which came to be known as the 'sledge hammer'.

George Hillyard, husband of Mrs. Hillyard, wrote of her that she gave the impression of not caring if she won in singles – in that aspect, he said, she was lazy. Commander Hillyard was the predecessor as All England Lawn Tennis Club Secretary to Dudley Larcome whom Ethel married in 1906. That period of duty, though, was not until 1925 to 1939, long after Ethel's peak playing days were over.

Lazy or not the champion of 1912 had a further distinction. She served underarm and was the last of the Wimbledon singles champions to do so.

She did not defend her title in 1913 because of another curious circumstance. Playing with Cecil Parke, the great Irish rugby man, in the final of the mixed doubles (which had that year become a fully fledged 'World Championship' event) she was struck in the eye from the ball mis-hit by her partner. They were a set up and 3–5 at the time. It not only cost her that title but the singles also, because she was out of action for some time and unable to defend her championship.

Ethel was 33 when she gained the singles. She competed for the last time in 1919, losing to Suzanne Lenglen, when aged 40. She became a coaching professional in 1922.

## Wimbledon Singles Record:

1902, won 0 matches, lost Agnes Morton, 1st round.

1903, won 4 matches, lost Dorothea Douglass, All Comers' Final.

1904, won 1 match, lost Agnes Morton, 3rd round.

1905, won 3 matches, lost May Sutton, quarter-final.

1906, won 0 matches, lost Dorothea Douglass, 2nd round.

1907–1911 did not play.

1912, won 4 matches, champion, (sets 8–1; games 56–25).

1913, did not play.

1914, won 5 matches, lost Dorothea Chambers, Challenge Round.

1919, won 1 match, lost Suzanne Lenglen, 2nd round.

**Matches:** 18–7; sets; 38–15; games; 287–185.

**Longest Match:** 3rd round 1904, lost to Agnes Morton 8–6 2–6 8–6 – a total of 36 games.

**Age on winning singles:** 33 years 30 days.

### Career Achievements:

The Championships, Wimbledon: singles 1912; mixed 1914.

Irish Championships: singles 1912; mixed 1912.

Scottish Championships: singles 1910, 1911, 1912; doubles 1910, 1911, 1912; mixed 1910, 1912.

**Full name:** Ethel Warneford Thomson/Larcombe

**Born:** 8th June, 1879, Islington, Middlesex, London.

**Married:** Dudley Larcombe on 15th October, 1906, Budleigh Salterton, Devon, England.

**Died:** 10th August, 1965, Budleigh Salterton, Devon, England, aged 86.

# Suzanne Lenglen

## 1919–1923, 1925

### The Champion Without a Peer

Suzanne Lenglen came first to Wimbledon in 1919 with a reputation that had been built before the four blank years of World War I. In Paris in 1914 at the age of 15 years 11 days she had won the World Hard Court Championship. She was new to grass.

Her Wimbledon initiation was story book. In the All-Comers' singles she was entirely dominant, losing no more than three games in any round save for a mildly testing 6–4 7–5 semi-final against Elizabeth Ryan. In the Challenge Round she opposed Dorothea Lambert Chambers who was defending a title she had won seven times since 1903. In the years immediately befor the war she had indisputably been the world's leading player.

Now aged 40 Mrs. Chambers resisted nobly. The Frenchwoman won a memorable final 10–8 4–6 9–7 after saving two match points. Watched by George V and Queen Mary she unlocked the door to her unique career.

Thereafter she was never beaten in a singles that went the full distance. Her utter invincibility was measured from the spring of 1914, when at St. Cloud she lost to her compatriot Marguerite Broquedis, to the summer of 1926 when she became a professional and ceased to play competitively.

One setback marred a record of perfection. It came at her only challenge in the U.S. Championships at Forest Hills in 1921. She had just got off the boat from Europe and, feeling unwell, she had to play her opening match against the best American, Molla Mallory. There was no seeding. Suzanne lost the first set 2–6 and half way through the next game could carry on no longer. Suzanne's response was in the Wimbledon final next year when she beat Mrs. Mallory 6–2 6–0 in 27 minutes.

Suzanne was at Wimbledon from 1919 to 1926. Only in 1924 did she again lose a set, this to Miss Ryan in the quarter-finals after winning three rounds without loss. She was ill and afterwards retired.

With Miss Ryan she had a doubles partnership that was equally flawless. The only matches Suzanne lost at Wimbledon were in the mixed doubles (to Randolph Lycett and Miss Ryan on two occasions) and once when partnering Didi Vlasto, a compatriot, in the ladies' doubles.

With her sparkling Gallic personality, her daringly short skirts, her balletic leaps about the court and her awesome capacity to control the ball within an inch or two, she became a legend. Crowds flocked to see her and because of her appeal there were few doubts that the expensive move of the All England Lawn Tennis Club from Worple Road to its new site in Church Road in 1922 would be justified.

Her superiority over all rivals grew more overwhelming. It reached a climax in 1925 when in her five rounds of singles Suzanne yielded a total of but five games. She was triple champion that year as in 1920 and 1922.

The traumatic year for Suzanne was 1926. In her own French Championships she won the singles for the loss of four games in five rounds. But at Wimbledon her imperious temperament clashed with the authoritarian control of Wimbledon's most famous referee, Frank Burrow. There was a misunderstanding about the time she should play. The crowd were incensed that their former idol had apparently been discourteous to Queen Mary who had come to watch. Suzanne stormed out of Wimbledon and never came back to the amateur game.

*Suzanne Lenglen*

Her father was her mentor and trainer throughout. After turning professional she toured for a time and later opened a lawn tennis school in France.

At least eight times in her career she won a tournament without losing any games at all in singles.

She had a famous clash with Helen Wills in the final of the Carlton tournament in 1926. She won 6–3 8–6. In 1994 a statue was unveiled to her at Roland Garros and the new 10,000 seat Suzanne Lenglen court was opened. Appropriately the street leading to her club in Nice is named after her.

**Wimbledon Singles Record:**
1919, won 7 matches, champion, (sets 14–1; games 96–38).
1920, won 1 match, champion, (sets 2–0; games 12–3)
1921, won 1 match, champion, (sets 2–0; games 12–2).
1922, won 6 matches, champion, (sets 12–0; games 75–20).
1923, won 6 matches, champion, (sets 12–0; games 72–11).
1924, won 4 matches, retired semi-final.
1925, won 5 matches, champion, (sets 10–0; games 60–5).
1926, won 2 matches, retired 3rd round.

**Matches:** 32–0; sets 64–2; games 405–102.

**Longest Match:** Challenge Round 1919, beat Dorothea Chambers 10–8 4–6 9–7 – a total of 44 games.

**Age on first winning singles:** 20 years 44 days.

**Age on last winning singles:** 26 years 42 days.

**Overall Record:**

|         | Titles | Matches Played | Won | Lost |
|---------|--------|--------|-----|------|
| Singles | 6      | 32     | 32  | 0    |
| Doubles | 6      | 31     | 30  | 1    |
| Mixed   | 3      | 31     | 29  | 2    |
| Total   | 15     | 94     | 91  | 3    |

**Career Achievements:**
*The Championships, Wimbledon:* singles 1919, 1920, 1921, 1922, 1923, 1925; doubles 1919, 1920, 1921, 1922, 1923, 1925; mixed 1920, 1922, 1925.
*French Championships:* singles 1920, 1921, 1922, 1923, 1925, 1926; doubles 1920, 1921, 1922, 1923, 1925, 1926; mixed 1914, 1920, 1921, 1922, 1923, 1925, 1926.
*World Hard Court Championships:* singles 1914, 1921, 1922, 1923; doubles 1914, 1921, 1922; mixed 1921, 1922, 1923.
*Olympic Games:* singles, 1920 gold; Mixed, 1920 gold.

**Full name:** Suzanne Rachel Flore Lenglen
**Born:** 24th May, 1899, Paris, France.
**Died:** 4th July, 1938, Paris, France, aged 39.

# Kathleen McKane/Godfree

## 1924, 1926

### British and Best

There were several unique aspects about the career of the greatest British woman player of the early 1920s. Kathleen McKane, as she originally was, won the first of her two singles in 1924. Yet in that year both Suzanne Lenglen and Helen Wills, the invincible players of the between-wars years, were challengers at Wimbledon.

An improbable feat it may have been when viewed in the light of history but it was none-the-less like that. The 1924 meeting was the only Wimbledon championship in which both Suzanne Lenglen and the then Miss Wills entered. There was no seeding then but the draw was such that they should have met in the final.

It was not in fact until two years later, 1926, that the two immortals had their famous clash at Cannes. But Suzanne Lenglen, having reached the semi-finals, had to scratch because of illness and Kathleen received a walkover.

In the final she met Miss Wills. It was the American's first Wimbledon. She was 18 but already U.S. National Champion. Kathleen beat her in a famous match, 4–6 6–4 6–4 after trailing 1–4 in the second set.

In retrospect it was a monumental outcome. It was the only singles defeat suffered at Wimbledon by the immortal 'Poker Faced' Helen, who won for the eighth time in 1938.

Two years later Mrs. Godfree, as Kathleen had become, won again. This time she was expected to meet Suzanne Lenglen in the final. That never came about since just before that the Frenchwoman had scratched from all events and walked out of Wimbledon for good. So Kathleen had an easier task against the grace and power of the Spaniard, Lili de Alvarez. But in the mixed doubles she achieved a feat which was unique then and has remained so since. She won with her husband Leslie Godfree.

Kitty, as she was popularly known, had prowess in other sports, notably badminton. She was All England Singles Champion four times, 1920–1922, 1924.

**Wimbledon Singles Record:**

1919, won 3 matches, lost Suzanne Lenglen, quarter-final.

1920, won 1 match, lost Winifred McNair, 3rd round.

1921, won 1 match, lost Elizabeth Ryan, 2nd round.

1922, won 1 match, lost Suzanne Lenglen, 2nd round.

1923, won 6 matches, lost Suzanne Lenglen, final.

1924, won 5 matches, champion, (sets 10–3; games 72–37).

1925, won 4 matches, lost Suzanne Lenglen, semi-final.

1926, won 6 matches, champion, (sets 12–2; games 77–29).

1927, seeded 2, won 3 matches, lost Elizabeth Ryan, quarter-final.

1928, 1929, did not play.

1930, played doubles only.
1931, unseeded, won 3 matches, lost Helen Jacobs, 4th round.
1932, unseeded, won 2 matches, lost Helen Moody, 4th round.
1933, unseeded, won 1 match, lost Peggy Scriven, 2nd round.
1934, unseeded, won 2 matches, lost Sarah Palfrey, 3rd round.

**Matches:** 38–11; sets 79–32; games 564–350.

**Longest Match:** 2nd round 1932, beat Elsa Haylock 6–2 6–8 6–3 – a total of 31 games.

**Age on first winning singles:** 28 years 58 days

**Age on last winning singles:** 30 years 57 days.

**Overall Record:**

|  | Titles | Matches | | |
|---|---|---|---|---|
|  |  | Played | Won | Lost |
| Singles | 2 | 49 | 8 | 11 |
| Doubles | 0 | 45 | 33 | 12 |
| Mixed | 2 | 52 | 40 | 12 |
| Total: | 4 | 146 | 111 | 35 |

**Career Achievements:**
*The Championships, Wimbledon:* singles 1924, 1926; mixed 1924, 1926.
*U.S. Championships:* doubles 1923, 1927; mixed 1925.
*Total Grand Slam titles:* 7 – singles 2, doubles 2, mixed 3.
*World Hard Court Championships:* doubles 1923.
*Olympic Games:* singles, 1920, 1924 bronze; doubles, 1920, gold, 1924 silver; mixed, 1920, silver, 1924, bronze.
*British Wightman Cup team:* 1923–1927, 1930, 1934, winning 7 from 17 matches in 7 ties (singles 5–5; doubles 2–5).

**Full name:** Kathleen McKane/Godfree
**Born:** 7th May, 1896, Bayswater, London, England.
**Married:** Leslie Godfree on 18th January, 1926, Kimberley, South Africa.
**Died:** 19th June, 1992, Barnes, London, England, aged 96.

# Helen Wills/Moody

1927–1930, 1932, 1933, 1935, 1938

## *Ice-cool and Invincible*

For over fifty years Helen Wills Moody's record of winning eight Wimbledon singles stood. She lost only at her first attempt in 1924 when, aged 18 and already U.S. Champion, she was beaten 6–4 4–6 4–6 after leading 4–1 in the second set by Britain's Kitty McKane. She won when she returned in 1927 and she went on winning every time she came back, the last in 1938 when she was 32.

On the court she was as efficient as a machine with a depth and pace of drive that was never broken down. She never showed emotion. Her soubriquet was 'Poker Faced Helen' and nothing could have been more apt.

She was almost, but not quite, as invincible as Suzanne Lenglen, whom she succeeded as queen of lawn tennis. In the autumn of 1926 she was beaten by Molla Mallory at Rye, New York. From that she measured seven years invulnerability for her next defeat was not until the final of the U.S. Championships in August 1933.

During those seven years she won Wimbledon six times, the U.S. title four times and the French Championships four times also. She also won 12 singles in the Wightman Cup.

As to that U.S. final defeat in 1933 the measure was 6–8 6–3 0–3 retired against her most noted rival, her fellow Californian Helen Jacobs. Helen was sick and had to give up. It was not until 1935 that a rival won a match point against her. That was at the Beckenham tournament in June when Britain's left-hander Kay Stammers beat her 6–0 6–4.

Helen did not lose a single set in singles from June 1927 (when she took three sets to beat Britain's Gwen Sterry in her opening match at Wimbledon) until the Wimbledon final of 1933 when Dorothy Round took her the full distance.

Year after year she measured her remorseless efficiency uneventfully. She reached her Wimbledon peak in 1932 when she won 72 games to 13 and had her worst performance in the final by 6–3 6–1 against Helen Jacobs.

The crises of her Wimbledon progress were few. There was her loss in the final in her apprentice year when she could carry a winning lead of 4–1 no further. In 1933 she was pressed to win the final by 6–4 6–8 6–3 against the patriotic surge of Miss Round.

Her next year, 1935, was momentous. In the fourth round a very young Czech, Lena Cepkova, lost her nerve and inspiration when a set in front and within a point of leading 4–1. There was the sight of a great champion playing badly and yet winning. Such happenings were hardly known to Helen.

The final brought Helen Jacobs to within a point of winning. Such a victory would have fulfilled a life-long ambition and given Helen Jacobs, a neighbour of Helen in Berkeley, a reward for which she had worked year after year. The rivalry between the 'two Helens' was a legend.

But Miss Jacobs, 5–3 ahead in the final set, was denied. She stood at match point and then had won the next rally – except for the formality of putting away the easiest of smashes no more than a yard from the net. But the falling ball was deflected slightly by the breeze. That and her nervousness made Miss Jacobs net the ball. Helen survived to win 6–3 3–6 7–5.

She did not come back to Wimbledon for another three years. She had some long sets (notably one of 12–10 in the semi-finals against Hilde Sperling) but her eighth title in 1938 was not her most difficult.

For more than a decade Helen set a standard that her rivals could only approach, never equal. If she never smiled she never frowned. She was an artist of no small accomplishment and held several exhibitions of her work.

**Wimbledon Singles Record:**
1924, won 5 matches, lost Kathleen McKane, final.
1925, 1926, did not play.
1927, seeded 1, won 7 matches, champion, (sets 14–1; games 74–27).
1928, seeded 1, won 6 matches, champion, (sets 12–0; games 72–18).
1929, seeded 1, won 6 matches, champion, (sets 12–0; games 72–16).
1930, seeded 1, won 6 matches, champion, (sets 12–0; games 72–19).
1931, did not play.
1932, seeded 1, won 6 matches, champion, (sets 12–0; games 72–13).
1933, seeded 1 , won 6 matches, champion, (sets 12–1; games 78–33).
1934, did not play.
1935, seeded 4, won 7 matches, champion, (sets 14–2; games 92–47).
1936, 1937 did not play.
1938, seeded 1, won 6 matches, champion, (sets 12–0; games 81–47).

**Matches:** 55–1; sets 111–6; games 701–263.

**Longest Match:** Final 1933, beat Dorothy Round 6–4 6–8 6–3 – a total of 33 games.

**Age on first winning singles:** 21 years 270 days.

**Age on last winning singles:** 32 years 270 days.

**Overall Record:**

| | Titles | Matches | | |
| --- | --- | --- | --- | --- |
| | | Played | Won | Lost |
| Singles | 8 | 56 | 55 | 1 |
| Doubles | 3 | 19 | 18 | 1 |
| Mixed | 1 | 22 | 19 | 3 |
| Total | 12 | 97 | 92 | 5 |

**Career Achievements:**

*The Championships, Wimbledon:* singles 1927, 1928, 1929, 1930, 1932, 1933, 1935, 1938; doubles 1924, 1927, 1930; mixed 1929.

*US Championships:* singles 1923, 1924, 1925, 1927, 1928, 1929, 1931; doubles 1922, 1924, 1925, 1928; mixed 1924, 1928.

*French Championships:* singles 1928, 1929, 1930, 1932; doubles 1930, 1932.

*Total Grand Slam titles:* 31 – singles 19, doubles 9, mixed 3.

*Olympic Games:* singles, 1924 gold ; doubles, 1924 gold.

*US Wightman Cup Team:* 1923–1925, 1929–1932, 1938, winning 21 from 30 matches in 10 ties (singles 18–2; doubles 3–7).

**Full name:** Helen Newington Wills/Moody/Roark

**Born:** 6th October, 1905, Centerville, Alameda Country, California, USA.

**Married:** Frederick Moody on 23rd December, 1929, Berkeley, California, USA; Aidan Roark on 28th October, 1939, Las Vegas, Nevada, USA.

**Died:** 1st January, 1998, Carmel, California, USA, aged 92.

# Cilly Aussem

## 1931

### *Germany Triumphant*

In 1931 Cilly Aussem was the first German to win a singles title at Wimbledon. It was a year when the absence of Helen Wills Moody, champion of the four previous years, had left a vacuum of talent. The challenge from Germany was never stronger and Cilly, seeded one by virtue of her status as champion of France, met her compatriot Hilde Krahwinkel, the fourth seed, in the final.

The graceful Cilly was competing for the fifth time. She could easily have been the finalist the year before, 1930, when she reached the semi-finals against Elizabeth Ryan. In her terms the score was 3–6 6–0 4 all when she sprained her ankle and dramatically had to be carried from the court on a stretcher. (It was the first year, incidentally, that no British woman reached the last four of the singles.)

1931 was Cilly's peak year. Subsequently she was bedevilled with ill health and did not compete at Wimbledon after 1934.

**Wimbledon Singles Record:**
1927, unseeded, won 0 matches, lost Betty Nuthall, 2nd round.
1928, seeded 7, won 3 matches, lost Lili d'Alvarez, quarter-final.
1929, seeded 8, won 2 matches, lost Joan Ridley, 4th round.
1930, seeded 6, won 4 matches, lost Elizabeth Ryan, semi-final.
1931, seeded 1, won 6 matches, champion, (sets 12–2; games 77–37).
1932, 1933, did not compete.
1934, seeded 7, won 4 matches, lost Helen Jacobs, quarter-final.

**Matches:** 19–5; sets; 39–13; games; 273–153.

**Longest Match:** 4th round 1928, beat Joan Strawson 6–1 4–6 6–1 – a total of 24 games.

**Age on winning singles:** 22 years 180 days.

**Overall Record:**

| | Titles | Matches Played | Won | Lost |
|---|---|---|---|---|
| Singles | 1 | 24 | 19 | 5 |
| Doubles | 0 | 5 | 1 | 4 |
| Mixed | 0 | 9 | 5 | 4 |
| Total | 1 | 38 | 25 | 13 |

**Career Achievements:**
*The Championships, Wimbledon:* singles 1931.
*French Championships:* singles 1931; mixed 1930.
*Total Grand Slam titles:* 3 – singles 2, mixed 1.
*German Championships:* singles 1927, 1930, 1931; mixed 1926, 1928, 1935.

**Full name:** Cilly Aussem/della Corte Brae
**Born:** 4th January, 1909, Cologne, Germany.
**Married:** Count Fermo della Corte Brae on 11th March, 1936, Berg, Starnberger See, Germany.
**Died:** 22nd March, 1963, Portofino, Genoa, Italy, aged 54.

# Dorothy Round

## 1934, 1937

## *The British Stayer*

The roots of lawn tennis go deep in the Midlands and Dorothy Round was born and bred in Dudley, Worcestershire, not all that far from Edgbaston where Major Harry Gem played his version of the game with his friends or from Leamington where the world's first lawn tennis club was founded in 1872.

Dorothy shares with Kitty Godfree the distinction of providing a British Ladies' Singles winner between the wars. There were no others and, like Mrs. Godfree, Dorothy won twice.

A distinguished junior in her own *milieux*, Dorothy first played in The Championships in 1928 at the age of 18. A steady rather than a mercurial player, albeit with more weight of drive than most, she improved her performance year by year, reaching the quarter-finals in 1931. Seeded eighth in 1932 she lost to Helen Wills Moody at the same stage. A year later she stood as the leading British player, was seeded second, and distinguished herself hugely by winning the middle set from Mrs. Moody in the final. It was the first set gleaned from the American since 1927.

With the invincible champion absent in 1934 Dorothy won at her 7th attempt. It coincided with the victory of Fred Perry in the Gentlemen's Singles to provide the most patriotically stimulating Championships since the early days of the century.

Her next two challenges were disappointing in that she got no further than the quarter-finals, despite her top seeding in both years. In 1937, this time seeded as low as seventh, she won again this time for the loss of one set in the final against the Polish Jadwiga Jedrzejowska. After marriage to Dr. Douglas Little, another Midlander, she did not defend her title in 1938 and appeared for the last time in 1939.

Her forte was in singles and her performance in doubles was not outstanding – save for the mixed doubles, where she was Wimbledon champion in three successive years, 1934 to 1936, first with the Japanese Ryuki Miki and twice with Perry.

Britain produced no such effective woman player as the resolute Dorothy for 24 years after her last triumph. The popular press made much of her avocation as a Sunday School teacher and her refusal to compete on the Sabbath.

**Wimbledon Singles Record:**

1928, unseeded, won 0 matches, lost Naomi Trentham, 1st round.

1929, unseeded, won 1 match, lost Betty Nuthall, 2nd round.

1930, unseeded, won 1 match, lost Freda James, 3rd round.

1931, unseeded, won 3 matches, lost Hilde Krahwinkel, quarter-final.

1932, seeded 8, won 3 matches, lost Helen Moody, quarter-final.

1933, seeded 2, won 5 matches, lost Helen Moody, final.

1934, seeded 2, won 7 matches, champion, (sets 12–1; games 75–29).

1935, seeded 1, won 3 matches, lost Joan Hartigan, quarter-final.

1936, seeded 1, won 3 matches, lost Hilde Sperling, quarter-final.

1937, seeded 7, won 6 matches, champion, (sets 12–1; games 75–29).

1938, did not play.

1939, unseeded, won 3 matches, lost Sarah Fabyan, 4th round.

**Matches:** 35–9; sets 74–26; games; 541–348.

**Longest Match:** 1st round 1928, lost to Naomi Trentham 6–2 6–8 8–6 – a total of 36 games.

**Age on first winning singles:** 24 years 359 days.

**Age on last winning singles:** 27 years 355 days.

**Overall Record:**

|  | Titles | Matches Played | Won | Lost |
|---|---|---|---|---|
| Singles | 2 | 44 | 35 | 9 |
| Doubles | 0 | 29 | 19 | 10 |
| Mixed | 3 | 34 | 27 | 7 |
| Total | 5 | 107 | 81 | 26 |

**Career Achievements:**

*The Championships, Wimbledon:* singles 1934, 1937; mixed 1934, 1935, 1936.
*Australian Championships:* singles 1935.
*Total Grand Slam titles:* 6 – singles 3, mixed 3.
*British Wightman Cup Team:* 1931–1936, winning 4 from 13 matches in 6 ties (singles 4–7; doubles 0–2).

**Full name:** Dorothy Edith Round/Little
**Born:** 13th July, 1909, Dudley, Worcestershire, England.
**Married:** Douglas Little on 2nd September, 1937, Dudley, Worcestershire, England.
**Died:** 12th November, 1982, Kidderminster, Worcestershire, England, aged 73.

# Helen Jacobs

## 1936

## Ambition Thwarted

If there were design to the pattern of lawn tennis in the decade spanning 1930 the *motif* would be the rivalry of the 'Two Helens' – the peerless Helen Wills Moody and her fellow Californian Helen Jacobs. They were close neighbours in Berkeley and Helen Jacobs was the younger by three years.

That there was bitterness in the rivalry owed more to the imagination of the writers of that time than to the facts; that Helen's career was largely taken up in trying without success to assail a rather stronger player is certain. For years they occupied the positions of the best women in the world and always – or nearly always – Mrs. Moody took top place.

The one occasion when Helen came out best was bitter-sweet. They met in the U.S. Championships singles final; at Forest Hills in 1933. Up to that stage Helen had played her rival seven times and never won a set. On this occasion she performed superbly, never more sure, never more adept. She favoured the chopped drive. She volleyed the more. She built a lead of 8–6 3–6 3–love when at the change-over Mrs. Moody quietly told the umpire that her legs were so weak she would have to retire.

Thus was the glory of a decisive win not achieved. But the next time Helen poised to fulfill her goal was heart breaking. They met in the Wimbledon final of 1935, the third of their clashes at that juncture. This was the year Mrs. Moody had shed some of her invulnerability. Helen took advantage of it. In the third set she advanced to 5–3 and then match point.

Helen advanced to the net to administer the *coup de grace*. Mrs Moody had almost been beaten by her forcing shot and had sent up a very short lob that was asking to be killed. As Helen shaped to smash, the breeze deflected the falling ball by just a fraction. That and her nervous tension sufficed to make her net the ball. Mrs. Moody then swept to victory.

Thus was Helen thwarted in her ambition. In all she played Mrs. Moody four times at Wimbledon, always in the final. She lost to her in the French Championships final of 1930 and had done so in the U.S. final of 1928. Helen also lost the French final to Peggy Scriven in 1934 and the U.S. finals of 1936 and 1939 to Alice

Marble. She had nine losing finals in the major events. Her solace was to win Wimbledon the once, in 1936, and to win the American title four times.

But only in 1933 at Forest Hills did she win when Mrs. Moody was in the same field.

She competed at Wimbledon first in 1928 and played every year until the Second World War. Only in that first year did she not reach at least the quarter-finals; she was five times the losing finalist.

**Wimbledon Singles Record:**
1928, seed 8, won 1 match, lost Daphne Akhurst, 3rd round.
1929, seeded 5, won 6 matches, lost Helen Wills, final.
1930, seeded 3, won 3 matches, lost Cilly Aussem, quarter-final.
1931, seeded 6, won 4 matches, lost Hilde Krahwinkel, semi-final.
1932, seeded 5, won 6 matches, lost Helen Moody, final.
1933, seeded 5, won 5 matches, lost Dorothy Round, semi-final.
1934, seeded 1, won 6 matches, lost Dorothy Round, final.
1935, seeded 3, won 6 matches, lost Helen Moody, final.
1936, seeded 2, won 6 matches, champion, (sets 12–2; games 78–40).
1937, seeded 1, won 3 matches, lost Dorothy Round, quarter-final.
1938, unseeded, won 6 matches, lost Helen Moody, final.
1939, seeded 2, won 3 matches, lost Kay Stammers, quarter-final.

**Matches:** 55–11; sets 111–26; games 751–402.

**Longest Match:** 3rd round 1928, lost to Daphne Akhurst 6–8 6–1 8–6 – a total of 35 games.

**Age on winning singles:** 27 years 333 days.

**Overall Record:**

| | Titles | Matches | | |
| | | Played | Won | Lost |
|---|---|---|---|---|
| Singles | 1 | 66 | 55 | 11 |
| Doubles | 0 | 26 | 18 | 8 |
| Mixed | 0 | 17 | 10 | 7 |
| Total | 1 | 109 | 83 | 26 |

**Career Achievements:**
*The Championships, Wimbledon:* singles 1936.
*US Championships:* singles 1932, 1933, 1934, 1935; doubles 1932, 1934, 1935; mixed 1934.
*Total Grand Slam titles:* 9 – singles 5, doubles 3, mixed 1.
*US Wightman Cup team:* 1927–1937, 1939 winning 19 from 30 matches in 12 ties (singles 14–8; doubles 5–3).

**Full name:** Helen Hull Jacobs
**Born:** 6th August, 1908, Globe, Arizona, U.S.A.
**Died:** 2nd June, 1997, Easthampton, New York, U.S.A., aged 88.

# Alice Marble

## 1939

### The Aggressive Invalid

Women's lawn tennis can be put into two eras, before Alice Marble and after. This Californian won her only Wimbledon singles title in 1939. The legacy she left ensured that when her American successors came back to the international scene after the interruption of the Second World War they were a new breed of player. After 1946 the capacity of women to serve and volley, to a degree undreamed of hitherto, was a basic fact of lawn tennis life.

Alice came to occupy her unique seminal status in the game after adversity that would have killed the hopes of lesser players. She had, it seemed, broken through to the world game when in 1934 she was chosen for the U.S. team going to Europe. The first fixture was an international match against France at the Stade Roland Garros. The 20 year old Alice collapsed while playing against Sylvia Henrotin. Tuberculosis was diagnosed and she was told she would never play again.

After two years she came back. Spectacularly – both because of her brief shorts and the virility of her net play – she won the U.S. singles at Forest Hills.

Alice came first to Great Britain in 1937. The ultimate success at first eluded her. She lost in the Wimbledon semi-finals to the Pole Jadwiga Jedrzejowska and since it was her third successive loss against her the pundits declared that the accepted principle of the efficient woman baseliner always beating the efficient woman volleyer was proven yet again.

In 1938 she again fell in the semi-finals, this time to her compatriot Helen Jacobs with a volleying ability well above the average. In 1937 she had won the mixed with Don Budge. She did so again and took the ladies' doubles as well with Sarah Fabyan.

Having thus taken first one Wimbledon title and then two Alice made a glorious triple crown of it in 1939. Her singles triumph was particularly impressive, for she lost no set, dropping only 21 games in her six rounds. Her victory in the final against Britain's left- hander, Kay Menzies, by 6–2 6–0 was the most one-sided at that stage since the Frenchwoman Suzanne Lenglen's success by the same score in 1925.

One can only assume that had it not been for the war Alice would have commanded the international game for some years. As it was she won her own U.S. National title up to 1940. She became a professional and when she subsequently played again in Great Britain, it was on the boards at Wembley.

Despite her illness and despite the war Alice ranks clearly as one of the game's immortals. She created the women's game in its aggressive modern style.

**Wimbledon Singles Record:**
1937, seeded 5, won 4 matches, lost Jadwiga Jedrzejowska, semi-final.
1938, seeded 2, won 4 matches, lost Helen Jacobs, semi-final.
1939, seeded 1, won 6 matches, champion, (sets 12–0; games 72–21).

**Matches:** 14–2; sets 28–6; games 197–102.

**Longest Match:** 2nd round 1938, beat Mary Hardwick 9–11 6–4 6–3 – a total of 39 games.

**Age on winning singles:** 25 years 293 days.

**Overall Record:**

|  | Titles | Matches Played | Won | Lost |
|---|---|---|---|---|
| Singles | 1 | 16 | 14 | 2 |
| Doubles | 2 | 10 | 9 | 1 |
| Mixed | 3 | 18 | 18 | 0 |
| Total | 6 | 44 | 41 | 3 |

**Career Achievements:**
*The Championships, Wimbledon:* singles 1939; doubles 1938, 1939; mixed 1937, 1938, 1939.
*US Championships:* singles 1936, 1938, 1939; doubles 1937, 1938, 1939; mixed 1936, 1938, 1939, (1940 all three titles – wartime).
*Total Grand Slam titles:* 15 – singles 4, doubles 5, mixed 6.
*US Wightman Cup team:* 1933, 1937–1939, winning 8 out of 10 matches in 4 ties (singles 5–1; doubles 3–1).

**Full name:** Alice Marble
**Born:** 28th September, 1913, Plumas County, California, U.S.A.
**Died:** 13th December, 1990, Palm Springs, California, U.S.A., aged 77.

# Pauline Betz

## 1946

### Brief Excellence

There are four women among the singles champions who were never beaten in that event at any time, Lottie Dod, Suzanne Lenglen, Pauline Betz and Maureen Connolly. In this restricted class Pauline is unique, for only she never lost a set.

One would not claim that this puts her above the others for she was the champion on only the one occasion, 1946. But in the rag-bag of might-have-beens in Wimbledon's history how many times might this superb player not have won if only things had turned out differently?

When in 1946 the American Wightman Cup side descended on the British game after the interruption of the war the standard of all of them was a revelation. Every one of them was destined to win the Wimbledon singles – Pauline, Margaret Osborne, Louise Brough and Doris Hart. And if the last three seem better known it is because in the records after 1946 Pauline's name disappeared. How ironic that was!

She was the complete player and moved flawlessly. She was dashing and secure. She won her six Wimbledon singles with impeccable play and her 6–2 6–4 outcome in the final against her compatriot Louise Brough was her closest match.

But having won Wimbledon and having gone home and won the U.S. National Singles and proved herself indisputably the best in the world she was some months after, asked if she would turn professional. The mere fact that she had discussed the proposition was sufficient in those days to make the U.S. Association declare she had infringed the amateur status. So, willy nilly, Pauline found herself a professional. Wimbledon never saw her grace again.

She was 26 when she won the singles. The speculation of might-have-beens may be taken back from 1946 since her peak years would obviously have been in the war. Of the war time U.S. Championships, which continued without interruption, Pauline won in 1942, 1943 and 1944.

So Pauline stands as one of the greatest players to whom the world's stage was denied. She became Mrs. Robert Addie in 1949.

## Wimbledon Singles Record:
1946, seeded 1, won 6 matches champion, (sets 12–0; games 72–20).

**Matches:** 6–0; sets 12–0; games; 72–20

**Longest Match:** 1946 final, beat Louise Brough 6–2 6–4 – a total of 18 games.

**Age on winning singles:** 26 years 344 days

**Overall Record:**

|  | Title | Matches | | |
|---|---|---|---|---|
|  |  | Played | Won | Lost |
| Singles | 1 | 6 | 6 | 0 |
| Doubles | 0 | 5 | 4 | 1 |
| Mixed | 0 | 6 | 5 | 1 |
| Total | 1 | 17 | 15 | 2 |

## Career Achievements:
*The Championships, Wimbledon:* singles 1946.
*U.S. Championships:* singles 1946. (1942, 1943, 1944 – wartime).
*French Championships:* mixed 1946.
*Total Grand Slam titles:* 3 – singles 2, mixed 1.
*U.S. Wightman Cup team:* 1946 winning 3 from 3 matches in 1 tie (singles 2–0, doubles 1–0).

**Full name:** Pauline May Betz/Addie
**Born:** 6th August, 1919, Drayton, Ohio, U.S.A.
**Married:** Robert Addie on 2nd February, 1949, Los Angeles, California, U.S.A.

# Margaret Osborne

## 1947

### American Efficiency

It is a curious fact of lawn tennis history that while Margaret Osborne was a very great player by any standard and worthy of standing on her own without a peer it is impossible to review her career without bringing in her comtemporary Louise Brough. In terms of Wimbledon achievement Miss Brough was the better. She won four singles titles to the one gained by Margaret.

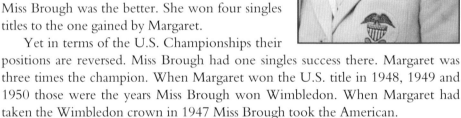

Yet in terms of the U.S. Championships their positions are reversed. Miss Brough had one singles success there. Margaret was three times the champion. When Margaret won the U.S. title in 1948, 1949 and 1950 those were the years Miss Brough won Wimbledon. When Margaret had taken the Wimbledon crown in 1947 Miss Brough took the American.

In harness as a doubles pair their joint record was astonishing. Together Miss Brough and Margaret won five times at Wimbledon. They won three times in France. For their own U.S. title they had an unparalleled sequence of nine consecutive victories from 1942 to 1950 and won again 1955 to 1957, to bring their total to 13 in all. Margaret's sequence was an original run of ten for her original doubles triumph for the U.S. crown was with Sarah Cooke in 1941.

Margaret was 23. In American terms she was a late developer. She first came to Wimbledon in 1946 as one of the band of players whose standards were a shattering revelation of American strength in depth. Pauline Betz was then the number one but when she fell out Margaret and Miss Brough vied for the succession.

In taking the Wimbledon singles in 1947 she lost a set to no-one and just one 7–5 set was the worst she had to weather. More exciting that year was her fate, with Miss Brough, in the ladies' doubles final. They were poised, after a splendid battle, to beat their compatriots Doris Hart and Pat Todd with a lead of 6–3 4–6 5–3, 40–love, with Miss Brough serving. With the spectators supporting the 'underdogs' it was the clamour and frenzy of the packed stands that lifted up and carried Miss Hart and Mrs. Todd to victory.

Margaret retired temporarily in 1952 and 1953, returned fleetingly in 1954 and then again in 1958 when she was no longer a serious player. None the less she reached the quarter-finals, her minimum singles achievement.

Remarkable in 1962 she made a striking last appearance. In singles she got nowhere, yielding to Britain's Christine Truman in the first round. But in her 'fun' event, the mixed doubles with the Australian left-hander, Neale Fraser, she won the mixed doubles, taking the final against Dennis Ralston and Ann Haydon 13–11 in the third set. At that time, Margaret, at 44 years, 125 days, was the oldest, man or woman, to have become a Wimbledon champion – a record which stood for over 40 years, when Martina Navratilova won the mixed title in 2003, aged 45 years, 261 days.

Margaret was born in Joseph, Oregon, but learned her game in San Francisco. She married William du Pont, a member of the notable Delaware family, but later separated.

**Wimbledon Singles Record:**
1946, seeded 2, won 4 matches, lost Louise Brough, semi-final.
1947, seeded 1, won 6 matches, champion, (sets 12–0; games 73–25).
1948, seeded 1 won 4 matches, lost Doris Hart, semi-final.
1949, seeded 2, won 5 matches, lost Louise Brough, final.
1950, seeded 2, won 5 matches, lost Louise Brough, final.
1951, seeded 2, won 3 matches, lost Beverley Baker, quarter-final.
1952, 1953, did not play.
1954, seeded 5, won 3 matches, lost Maureen Connolly, quarter-final.
1955–1957, did not play.
1958, unseeded, won 4 matches, lost Angela Mortimer, quarter-final.
1959–1961, did not play.
1962, unseeded, won 0 matches, lost Christine Truman, 1st round.

**Matches:** 34–8; sets 73–19; games 520–293

**Longest Match:** Final 1949, lost to Louise Brough 10–8 1–6 10–8 – a total of 43 games.

**Age on winning singles:** 29 years, 123 days.

**Overall Record:**

|  | Titles | Matches | | |
|---|---|---|---|---|
|  |  | Played | Won | Lost |
| Singles | 1 | 42 | 34 | 8 |
| Doubles | 5 | 42 | 38 | 4 |
| Mixed | 1 | 41 | 33 | 8 |
| Total | 7 | 125 | 105 | 20 |

**Career Achievements:**
*The Championships, Wimbledon:* singles 1947; doubles 1946, 1948, 1949, 1950, 1954; mixed 1962.
*U.S. Championships:* singles 1948, 1949, 1950; doubles 1946, 1947, 1948, 1949, 1950, 1955, 1956, 1957; mixed 1946, 1950, 1956, 1958, 1960. (1941, 1942, 1943, 1944, 1945 doubles and 1943, 1944 and 1945 mixed – wartime.)
*French Championships:* singles 1946, 1949: doubles 1946, 1947, 1949.
*Total Grand Slam titles:* 29 – singles 6, doubles 16, mixed 7.
*U.S. Wightman Cup team:* 1946–1950, 1954, 1955, 1957, 1962 winning 18 from 18 matches in 9 ties (singles 10–0; doubles 8–0).

**Full name:** Margaret Evelyn Osborne/du Pont
**Born:** 4th March, 1918, Joseph, Oregon, U.S.A.
**Married:** William du Pont on 26th November, 1947, Wilmington, Delaware, U.S.A.

# Louise Brough

1948–1950, 1955

## *Champion in Perpetual Motion*

To Louise Brough belongs the distinction of dominating The Championships for three successive years more completely than any other player before or since her time. In 1948, 1949 and 1950 she played all three events and but for a loss in the final of the mixed doubles in the middle year would have been triple champion three years running.

In the three meetings she took part in 51 matches. She won 50. On the final Saturday in 1948 she played three finals, won 47 games to 29. On the final Saturday in 1949 she again played eight sets and participated in 117 games, winning 59 and losing 58.

Such a day's work had never been achieved on the Centre Court before. Louise won her singles 10–8 1–6 10–8, her doubles with Margaret du Pont 8–6 7–5, and with John Bromwich lost the mixed 7–9 11–9 5–7 where 48 games made for the longest at that stage. She was on court more than 5 hours.

In 1950 she again played in all three finals and this time won them all. The effort was briefer than the year before and she won 50 games to 39 though every final was a three setter.

So in three successive final days Louise played nine finals, 25 sets and 282 games.

As early as the first post-war Wimbledon, 1946, she had accustomed herself to a full day on the final Saturday. She was a triple finalist then but lost the first, the singles to Pauline Betz. In the end she played seven sets and a total of 64 games, winning 32 and losing 32.

The sequence of 1948 to 1950, when she won eight titles at Wimbledon in three years, is matched only by Suzanne Lenglen for 1920 to 1922 but the Frenchwoman was not, like Louise, a triple finalist in the middle year.

The indefatigable Louise played every year from 1946 to 1957, save 1953, when she was absent. In singles she never did worse than the quarter-finals. She won her fourth title in 1955 at the age of 32 and did not lose a set.

As a doubles player she belonged inseparably with Margaret du Pont with whom she won Wimbledon five times and the U.S. title 12. But in the Wimbledon context she was the stronger mixed player and took the Championship four times with three different partners, Tom Brown, John Bromwich (twice) and Eric Sturgess.

Louise was born in Oklahoma City. She learned her lawn tennis in Los Angeles and belonged whole heartedly to the agressive, hard volleying Californian school. She must rank among the all time greats of the game.

**Wimbledon Singles Record:**

1946, seeded 3, won 5 matches, lost Pauline Betz, final.

1947, seeded 2, won 4 matches, lost Doris Hart, semi-final.

1948, seeded 2, won 6 matches, champion, (sets 11–1; games 70–29).

1949, seeded 1, won 6 matches, champion, (sets 12–1; games 81–36).

1950, seeded 1, won 6 matches, champion, (sets 12–2; games 80–33).

1951, seeded 1, won 4 matches, lost Shirley Fry, semi-final.

1952, seeded 4, won 6 matches, lost Maureen Connolly, final.

1953, did not play.

1954, seeded 4, won 6 matches, lost Maureen Connolly, final.

1955, seeded 2, won 6 matches, champion, (sets 12–0; games 77–28).

1956, seeded 1, won 4 matches, lost Shirley Fry, semi-final.

1957, seeded 2, won 3 matches, lost Darlene Hard, quarter-final.

**Matches:** 56–7; sets 113–24; games 776–372.

**Longest Match:** Final 1949, beat Margaret du Pont 10–8 1–6 10–8 – a toal of 43 games.

**Age on first winning singles:** 25 years 114 days.

**Age on last winning singles:** 32 years 113 days.

**Overall Record:**

|  | Titles | Matches Played | Won | Lost |
|---|---|---|---|---|
| Singles | 4 | 63 | 56 | 7 |
| Doubles | 5 | 43 | 39 | 4 |
| Mixed | 4 | 49 | 44 | 5 |
| Total | 13 | 155 | 139 | 16 |

**Career Achievements:**

*The Championships, Wimbledon:* singles 1948, 1949, 1950, 1955; doubles 1946, 1948, 1949, 1950, 1954; mixed 1946, 1947, 1948, 1950.

*U.S. Championships:* singles 1947; doubles 1946, 1947, 1948, 1949, 1950, 1955, 1956, 1957; mixed 1942, 1947, 1948, 1949. (1942, 1943, 1944, 1945 doubles – wartime.)

*French Championships:* doubles 1946, 1947, 1949.

*Australian Championships:* singles 1950; doubles 1950.

*Total Grand Slam titles:* 30 – ingles 6, doubles 17, mixed 7.

*U.S. Wightman Cup team:* 1946–1948, 1950, 1952–1957 winning 22 from 22 matches in 10 ties (singles 12–0; doubles 10–0).

**Full name:** Althea Louise Brough/Clapp

**Born:** 11th March, 1923, Oklahoma City, Oklahoma, U.S.A.

**Married:** Alan Clapp on 9th August, 1958, Santa Barbara, California, U.S.A.

# Doris Hart

## 1951

### *Style and Power*

Doris Hart was the fourth of that quartet of American players who had their formative years in wartime U.S.A. and who combined to form a standard of excellence surpassing anything seen before. The other three were Pauline Betz, Margaret du Pont and Louise Brough. In their company Doris ranked as an also ran. Had they not been there she would have been reckoned as one of the all time greats.

Only Miss Betz could match her stylish grace. Her easy mobility and flow of movement was the more remarkable since as a child she had been threatened with a crippling disease. She took to the lawn tennis court as part of her therapy and her right leg remained partially deformed.

Doris's grace on court was matched by a graciousness off it and her singles success at her fifth attempt in 1951 was very popular. She was triple champion, taking the doubles with Shirley Fry and the mixed with the Australian Frank Sedgman. The doubles she won for the next two years but she remained unbeaten in mixed doubles until she retired. She had two wins with Sedgman and three with Vic Seixas.

Her triple 1951 championship was forthright and she lost a set only in the mixed doubles. Two years later brought the most curious final result of all time in the ladies' doubles. In retaining their title Doris and Shirley Fry played the final against Maureen Connolly, outstandingly the best singles player in the world by that time, and Julie Sampson. They won 6–0 6–0.

Doris was never beaten in singles prior to the quarter-finals. Nor did she ever lose to any but an American.

She inflicted on Maureen Connolly two of the four defeats suffered by that otherwise invincible. In three successive years in the French Championships she played all three finals. She won seven. In the U.S. Nationals she was finalist in all three events for the four years 1952 to 1955, winning nine out of the 12 titles. In that event she played, from 1949 to 1955, 19 finals out of a possible 21. She was triple champion not only of Wimbledon but of France in 1952 and of the U.S.A. in 1954.

The prowess of Doris as a mixed player was exceptional. From 1951 she won the French title for the next three years, the Wimbledon mixed for the next five and the American for the next five also. She became a professional coach in 1955.

## Wimbledon Singles Record:

1946, seeded 7, won 3 matches, lost Margaret Osborne, quarter-final.
1947, seeded 3, won 6 matches, lost Margaret Osborne, final.
1948, seeded 4, won 6 matches, lost Louise Brough, final.
1949, did not play.
1950, seeded 3, won 5 matches, lost Louise Brough, semi-final.
1951, seeded 3, won 7 matches, champion, (sets 14–0; games 86–34).
1952, seeded 1, won 3 matches, lost Pat Todd, quarter-final.
1953, seeded 2, won 5 matches, lost Maureen Connolly, final.
1954, seeded 2, won 4 matches, lost Louise Brough, semi-final.
1955, seeded 1, won 4 matches, lost Beverly Fleitz, semi-final.
1968, played doubles only.

**Matches:** 43–8; sets 91–23; games 633–333.

**Longest Match:** Quarter-final 1952, lost to Pat Todd 6–8 7–5 6–4 – a total of 36 games.

**Age on winning singles:** 26 years 17 days.

## Overall Record:

|         | Titles | Matches | | |
|---------|--------|---------|-----|------|
|         |        | Played  | Won | Lost |
| Singles | 1      | 51      | 43  | 8    |
| Doubles | 4      | 42      | 36  | 6    |
| Mixed   | 5      | 52      | 47  | 5    |
| Total   | 10     | 145     | 126 | 19   |

## Career Achievements:

*The Championships, Wimbledon:* singles 1951; doubles 1947, 1951, 1952, 1953; mixed 1951, 1952, 1953, 1954, 1955.
*U.S. Championships:* singles 1954, 1955 doubles; 1951, 1952, 1953, 1954; mixed 1951, 1952, 1953, 1954, 1955.
*French Championships*: singles 1950, 1952; doubles 1948, 1950, 1951, 1952, 1953; mixed 1951, 1952, 1953.
*Australian Championships:* singles 1949; doubles 1950; mixed 1948, 1950.
*Total Grand Slam titles:* 35 – singles 6, doubles 14, mixed 15.
*Italian Championships:* singles 1951, 1953; doubles 1951; mixed 1953.
*U.S. Wightman Cup team:* 1946–1955, winning 22 from 24 matches in 10 ties (singles 14–1; doubles 8–1).

**Full name:** Doris Jane Hart
**Born:** 20th June, 1925, St. Louis, Missouri, U.S.A.

# Maureen Connolly

## 1952–1954

### The Precocious Paragon

In the history of lawn tennis there are three players, all women, who stand out because they were invincible or nearly so. Suzanne Lenglen was the first, Helen Wills Moody the second and Maureen Connolly was the third. Like Mrs. Moody she was Californian. Like Mlle Lenglen she died before her time, in her case at the age of 34.

Her career was sadly brief as well, not because of illness as such but because she broke her leg while riding. When she did so, in 1954 she was not yet 21.

She was 20 years old and had won the Wimbledon singles three times, the U.S. title three times, the French twice and the Australian once. In her international career she had lost just four times, twice to Doris Hart, to Shirley Fry and to Beverly Fleitz and at no time in a vital contest.

Nor had she, when she had to give up her career, fully developed as a player. Her remorseless invincibility was founded on the traditional accuracy and pace of her ground strokes. Indeed her backhand was probably the most punishing ever possessed by a woman. But her volleying, which had been virtually non-existent at the start, was still in the process of being created with the help of Australia's Davis Cup Captain, Harry Hopman.

Maureen broke through to the top of the women's game, where she stayed without the slightest hint of being moved, when at the age of 16 she won the U.S. singles at Forest Hills. That was 1951.

Her Wimbledon progress began in 1952, when 17. Her success in her initial year was almost melodramatic. She had come to England with her coach, Eleanor Tennant, as mentor and chaperone. On the eve of the tournament, which had been preceded by immaculate progress through Surbiton, Manchester and the Wightman Cup, she developed a sore shoulder. Miss Tennant advised withdrawal and was adamant. The inexperienced Maureen promptly dismissed her and called a press conference to announce the fact. Rarely was there such a wise head on such young shoulders.

The justification of her decision not to coddle herself was made apparent. Maureen went through the singles, not without scars, but with assured superiority in every round. Britain's Sue Partridge, adopting the ploy of giving her opponent little pace down the middle of the court, extended her to 7–5 in the third set in round four. In the quarter-finals the experienced Australian, Thelma Long, adopted like tactics and won the first set.

They were the only sets the peerless Maureen lost in the singles in her three year reign. In the final of 1953 Miss Hart stretched her to her full capacity (the score was 8–6 7–5) but the likelihood of defeat never loomed.

Yet her Wimbledon progress was marked by one of the most curious results in the story of the women's game. In 1953 Maureen was accompanied by the Californian Julie Sampson as chaperone. She was, after all, only 18. Julie Sampson was a fine player in her own right but perhaps not of international calibre. They partnered each other in the ladies' doubles.

They were seeded second and duly reached the final, where they met Shirley Fry and Doris Hart. There Miss Sampson's nerves failed her and Maureen's relative lack of expertise on the volley was made apparent. Miss Fry and Miss Hart won 6–0 6–0!

It was only the second time a whitewash had been effected in a Wimbledon final. It had occurred in the Ladies' Singles final of 1911 when Dorothea Chambers routed Dora Boothby.

This quirk of fate came in the course of Maureen's most spectacular achievement. In 1953 she won the Grand Slam, the first woman to hold all four major titles, those of Australia, France, Wimbledon and the U.S. in the same year.

She broke her leg immediately after winning the U.S. Clay Court title in 1954 and was unable to defend her U.S. National crown. She became a professional coach and married Norman Brinker. She died in Dallas leaving two young children, a victim of cancer and as young to die as she had been young to achieve so much.

**Wimbledon Singles Record:**
1952, seeded 2, won 6 matches, champion, (sets 12–2; games 84–48).
1953, seeded 1, won 6 matches, champion, (sets 12–0; games 75–19).
1954, seeded 1, won 6 matches, champion, (sets 12–0; games 73–19).

**Matches:** 18–0; sets 36–2; games 232–86.

**Longest Match:** 4th round 1952, beat Susan Partridge 6–3 5–7 7–5 – a total of 33 games.
**Age on first winning singles:** 17 years 292 days.

**Age on last winning singles:** 19 years 290 days.

**Overall Record:**

| | Titles | Matches Played | Won | Lost |
|---|---|---|---|---|
| Singles | 3 | 18 | 18 | 0 |
| Doubles | 0 | 9 | 7 | 2 |
| Mixed | 0 | 12 | 9 | 3 |
| Total | 3 | 39 | 34 | 5 |

**Career Achievements:**

*The Championships, Wimbledon:* singles 1952, 1953, 1954.

*U.S. Championships:* singles 1951, 1952, 1953.

*French Championships:* singles 1953, 1954; doubles 1954; mixed 1954.

*Australian Championships:* singles 1953; doubles 1953.

*Total Grand Slam titles:* 12 – singles 9, doubles 2, mixed 1.

*Grand Slam:* singles 1953

*Italian Championships:* singles 1954.

*U.S. Wightman Cup team:* 1951–1954, winning 9 from 9 matches in 4 ties (singles 7–0; doubles 2–0).

**Full name:** Maureen Catherine Connolly/Brinker

**Born:** 17th September, 1934, San Diego, California, U.S.A.

**Married:** Norman Brinker on 11th June, 1955, San Diego, California, U.S.A.

**Died:** 21st June, 1969, Dallas, Texas, U.S.A., aged 34.

# Shirley Fry

1956

## The Trier from Akron

Shirley Fry was from Akron, Ohio, and she first played at Wimbledon just before her 21st birthday in 1948. She would certainly have stood out more had it not been for the awesome talent of her fellow Americans, Louise Brough, Margaret Osborne and Doris Hart. Later her career overlapped that of Maureen Connolly and she was one of the three women who beat that prodigy – by 6–2 7–5 in the semi-finals of the Pacific South West Championships in Los Angeles in 1953.

At Wimbledon she had her reward in 1956. It was her eighth, and last, attempt in nine years. She was the fifth seed and there were two keys by which she unlocked the doors to her triumph. In the quarter-finals she beat the fourth seeded Althea Gibson, the powerful black American. In the semi-finals she was able to take advantage of the declining form of Louise Brough.

The final, as it turned out, was the least of her trials. There were curious happenings in the top half of the draw that year. It happened that the second seed – the first was Miss Brough – was the ambidexterous Beverly Fleitz, the former Miss Baker, then at the peak of her game. But Beverly Fleitz found herself in the position of having to consult the chairman of the Management Committee, Colin Gregory, who happened to be a doctor. He confirmed her suspicion that she was pregnant and she scratched in the quarter-finals to Britain's Angela Buxton. As it happened the other quarter-finals in that half brought an upset by Pat Ward over Angela Mortimer. In this all British gala Angela Buxton won her semi-final against Miss Ward to make for the first British Ladies' Singles finalist since Kay Stammers in 1939.

Shirley, winning 6–3 6–1, had the easiest final victory since she herself was routed at that stage by Doris Hart in 1951. She capped that performance by winning the mixed with Vic Seixas.

Shirley repeated her Wimbledon performance in her own national championships soon after. She then won the Australian title but made no attempt to hold all four Grand Slam titles by not competing at the French meeting. In 1957 she married Mr. Karl Irving and retired.

**Wimbledon Singles Record:**
1948, seeded 8, won 3 matches, lost Louise Brough, quarter-final.
1949, seeded 5, won 2 matches, lost Betty Hilton, 4th round.
1950, seeded 5, won 3 matches, lost Louise Brough, quarter-final.
1951, seeded 4, won 6 matches, lost Doris Hart, final.
1952, seeded 3, won 5 matches, lost Maureen Connolly, semi-final.
1953, seeded 3, won 4 matches, lost Maureen Connolly, semi-final.
1954, seeded 3, won 4 matches, lost Betty Pratt, quarter-final.
1955, did not play.
1956, seeded 5, won 7 matches, champion, (sets 14–2; games 92–49).

**Matches:** 34–7; sets 71–18; games 471–282.

**Longest Match:** Quarter-final 1954, lost to Betty Pratt 6–4 9–11 6–3 – a total of 39 games.

**Age on winning singles:** 29 years 7 days.

**Overall Record:**

|  | Titles | Matches | | |
| --- | --- | --- | --- | --- |
|  |  | Played | Won | Lost |
| Singles | 1 | 41 | 34 | 7 |
| Doubles | 3 | 35 | 31 | 4 |
| Mixed | 1 | 26 | 21 | 5 |
| Total | 5 | 102 | 86 | 16 |

**Career Achievements:**

*The Championships, Wimbledon:* singles 1956; doubles 1951, 1952, 1953; mixed 1956.
*U.S. Championships:* singles 1956; doubles 1951, 1952, 1953, 1954.
*French Championships:* singles 1951; doubles 1950, 1951, 1952, 1953.
*Australian Championships:* singles 1957; doubles 1957.
*Total Grand Slam titles:* 17 – singles 4, doubles 12, mixed 1.
*Italian Championships:* doubles 1951; mixed 1951.
*U.S. Wightman Cup team:* 1949, 1951–1953, 1955, 1956 winning 10 from 12 matches in 6
   ties (singles 4–2; doubles 6–0).

**Full name:** Shirley June Fry/Irvine
**Born:** 30th June, 1927, Akron, Ohio, U.S.A.
**Married:** Karl Irving on 16th February, 1957, Sydney, N.S.W., Australia.

# Althea Gibson

## 1957, 1958

### *The Black Bombshell*

Althea Gibson, the first black player to win a major lawn tennis championship, made a fleeting visit to Wimbledon in 1951 and won and lost a match. Originating from South Carolina at a time when the black communities laboured under many social hardships, she did not get on the international scene until she was in her 29th year.

That was in 1956 and she had but three years at the top level. Her inauguration was striking for she won singles and doubles in the French Championships. At Wimbledon she got no further than Shirley Fry in the quarter-finals. She also lost to Miss Fry in the final of the U.S. Championships at Forest Hills.

In 1957, however, the tall, powerful and athletic Althea had a meteoric year. Her athleticism presaged that of Margaret Court. On Wimbledon's grass she was overpowering and in the singles no rival extended her to advantage games. And, having won the doubles in 1956 with the British Angela Buxton, she took that title also in 1957 with the American Darlene Hard. She had it for the third time in 1958 with the Brazilian Maria Bueno.

She had the 1958 singles also, this time losing just one set, to Shirley Bloomer, in the quarters. In the run up to Wimbledon she had been less invincible, for it was her downfall to the young British heroine Christine Truman in the Wightman Cup that turned the key to the novelty of a British victory. But in The Championships she remained inviolate and so she was also in the U.S. title meeting.

Having thus won, in three years, five out of six possible titles at Wimbledon, and taken two out of the three singles finals she played at Forest Hills, Althea became a professional. She had pushed forward the frontiers of the increasingly masculine standards in the women's game.

She became Mrs. William Darben in 1965 and Mrs. Sydney Llewellyn in 1983. Her lawn tennis success belongs not only to the story of the game, but to the liberation of the American negro.

**Wimbledon Singles Record:**

1951, unseeded, won 1 match, lost Beverly Baker, 3rd round.

1956, seeded 4, won 4 matches, lost Shirley Fry, quarter-final.

1957, seeded 1, won 6 matches, champion, (sets 12–0; games 72–30).

1958, seeded 1, won 6 matches, champion, (sets 12–1; games 83–36).

**Matches:** 17–2; sets 35–7; games 238–126.

**Longest Match:** Quarter-final 1958, beat Shirley Bloomer 6–3 6–8 6–2 – a total of 31 games.

**Age on first winning singles:** 29 years 315 days.

**Age on last winning singles:** 30 years 314 days.

**Overall Record:**

|  | Titles | Matches Played | Won | Lost |
|---|---|---|---|---|
| Singles | 2 | 19 | 17 | 2 |
| Doubles | 3 | 15 | 15 | 0 |
| Mixed | 0 | 19 | 15 | 4 |
| Total | 5 | 53 | 47 | 6 |

**Career Achievements:**

*The Championships, Wimbledon:* singles 1957, 1958; doubles 1956, 1957, 1958.
*U.S. Championships:* singles 1957, 1958; mixed 1957.
*French Championships:* singles 1956; doubles 1956.
*Australian Championships:* doubles 1957.
*Total Grand Slam titles:* 11 – singles 5, doubles 5, mixed 1.
*U.S. Wightman Cup team:* 1957, 1958 winning 5 from 6 matches in 2 ties (singles 3–1; doubles 2–0).

**Full name:** Althea Gibson/Darben/Llewellyn
**Born:** 25th August, 1927, Silver, South Carolina, U.S.A.
**Married:** William Darben on 17th October, 1965, Las Vegas, Nevada, U.S.A.
    S. Llewellyn on 11th April, 1983, Elkton, Maryland, U.S.A.
**Died:** 20th September, 2003, East Orange, New Jersey, USA, aged 76.

# Maria Bueno

## 1959, 1960, 1964

## *Majestic Grace*

Maria Bueno, from Sao Paulo, was the only Brazilian woman to fill a role at the very top level of lawn tennis. That her resounding success inspired her compatriots to issue a postage stamp bearing her portrait was hardly to be wondered at. The majestic grace of her game, its fluidity, its economy of effort, its all round effectiveness brought admiration from beyond the confines of the sport.

She arrived on the international scene in 1958 at the age of 18 as a competitor in the Italian Championships in Rome. She won the singles, despite match points against her by the defending champion, Britain's Shirley Bloomer, in the quarter-finals.

Maria's impact at Wimbledon was immediate. She was seeded fourth and just failed to justify the placing when she lost in the quarter-finals to Ann Haydon. Then, as throughout her career, if her best touch was lacking she had small ability to compromise. It was, as it were, perfection or nothing.

She established her championship status at Wimbledon in 1959, at her second attempt and when only 19. She played with growing confidence and lost no set in the last three rounds. Having also won the U.S. title in 1959 she had her second triumph at Wimbledon in 1960, this time losing one set only, to Christine Truman in the semi-finals.

An attack of jaundice put her out of the game in 1961. She again found her immaculate form in 1964 when she won her third Wimbledon singles.

By this time the women's game had produced a rare trinity of excellence, for if Maria found her peak so did the Australian Margaret Smith and the American Billie Jean Moffitt. In 1964 Miss Smith beat Miss Moffitt in the semi-final and Maria, having disposed of the second Australian, Lesley Turner, in turn beat Miss Smith in a quality final, winning 6–4 7–9 6–3.

The following year Maria beat Miss Moffitt in the semi-finals, by 6–4 5–7 6–3 and again played the Australian for the title. Miss Smith had revenge and won 6–4 7–5 to be second time the champion. In 1966 Maria reached her third successive final – her fifth in all – Billie Jean King (as Miss Moffitt now was) the victor by 6–3 3–6 6–1.

The year 1966 also saw the last of Maria's doubles triumphs, this time with Nancy Richey. It was her fifth. Since 1958 she had won with Althea Gibson, twice with Darlene Hard and with Billie Jean Moffitt.

Her last year as a serious contender was the first of the Opens, 1968 when she was a quarter-finalist. She made subsequent visits in 1976, 1977 and 1980. In 1976 when she was 36 she was good enough to battle as far as the singles quarter-finals.

Her rivalry with the great Margaret Court, then Miss Smith, brought many notable clashes. Probably the most dramatic was the final of the Italian Championships in 1962 when Miss Smith won 8–6 5–7 6–4, athleticism beating grace after both those qualities had been brought to unparalleled heights. The Australian's career superiority over Maria 1960 to 1968 was measured by 16 wins to 6 losses. But it was Maria who had the better of the last meeting in a Grand Slam, the quarter-finals of the U.S. Open in 1968. The score was 7–5 2–6 6–3.

The artistry of Maria's style, marked by impeccable timing of ball and racket string, never ceased to entrance, especially in the setting of Wimbledon. In all she won 116 matches.

**Wimbledon Singles Record:**
1958, seeded 4, won 4 matches, lost Ann Haydon, quarter-final.
1959, seeded 6, won 7 matches, *champion,* (sets 14–2; games 94–48).
1960, seeded 1, won 6 matches, *champion,* (sets 12–1; games 79–26).
1961, did not play.
1962, seeded 3, won 5 matches, lost lost Vera Sukova, semi-final.
1963, seeded 7, won 3 matches, lost Billie Jean King, quarter-final.
1964, seeded 2, won 6 matches, *champion,* (sets 12–2; games 82–42).
1965, seeded 1, won 5 matches, lost Margaret Smith, final.
1966, seeded 2, won 5 matches, lost Billie Jean King, final.

1967, seeded 2, won 2 matches, lost Rosemary Casals, 4th round.
1968, seeded 6, won 3 matches, lost Nancy Richey, quarter-final.
1969–1975, did not play.
1976, unseeded, won 3 matches, lost Sue Barker, quarter-final.
1977, unseeded, won 1 match, lost Billie Jean King, 3rd round.
1978, 1979, did not play.
1980, played doubles only.

**Matches:** 50–9; sets 101–31; games 738–459.

**Longest Match:** Semi-final 1966, beat Ann Jones 6–3 9–11 7–5 – a total of 41 games.

**Age on first winning singles:** 19 years 266 days.

**Age on last winning singles:** 24 years 267 days.

**Overall Record:**

|  | Titles | Matches Played | Won | Lost |
|---|---|---|---|---|
| Singles | 3 | 59 | 50 | 9 |
| Doubles | 5 | 41 | 37 | 4 |
| Mixed | 0 | 37 | 29 | 8 |
| Total | 8 | 137 | 116 | 21 |

**Career Achievements:**
*The Championships, Wimbledon:* singles 1959, 1960, 1964; doubles 1958, 1960, 1963, 1965, 1966.
*U.S. Championships:* singles 1959, 1963, 1964, 1966; doubles 1960, 1962, 1966, 1968.
*French Championships:* doubles 1960; mixed 1960.
*Australian Championships:* doubles 1960.
*Total Grand Slam titles:* 19–singles 7; doubles 11; mixed 1.
*Grand Slam Doubles:* 1960 (Australian – Christine Truman, French, Wimbledon, USA – Darlene Hard)
*Italian Championships:* singles 1958, 1961, 1965; doubles 1962.
*Brazilian Federation Cup team:* 1965, 1976, 1977, winning 3 from 6 matches in 5 ties (singles 2–2; doubles 1–1)

**Full name:** Maria Esther Andion Bueno
**Born:** 11th October, 1939, Sao Paulo, Brazil.

# Angela Mortimer

## 1961

### *The British Revivalist*

Angela Mortimer was 29 years old and competing at Wimbledon for the 11th time in singles when in 1961 she emerged as the heroine of the most patriotic occasion there since Dorothy Round had captured the women's crown for Great Britain in 1937. That event, indeed, had not echoed with so loud a chauvinistic note for nearly fifty years.

The final in which Angela was involved was against Christine Truman, the first to be all British since 1914. Angela won an exciting match, losing the first set and trailing 3–4 and facing a break point in the second when the aggressive momentum of the opposition was checked by a fall.

Happenings went well for the home players that year. The overwhelming American strength had temporarily diminished. Three British women were seeded, Ann Haydon at three, Miss Truman at six and Angela at seven. When she won no champion had been seeded lower.

Angela was a stylist in the classic tradition, with splendid driving control and more than normal diligence. She had developed her game under the watchful eye of Arthur Roberts, the coach at the Palace Hotel, Torquay, where the two covered courts with a fast wood surface provided a continuity of training that few others enjoyed at that time. Two other Roberts' pupils, Michael Sangster and Sue Barker would later rise to prominence internationally.

Angela's first major international success was in taking the French Championship in 1955 when she survived the longest final at that stage, 2–6 7–5 10–8, against Dorothy Knode. Her capacity to play to the same level on fast grass was made evident when she won the Australian singles in 1958.

Later that year she had her best ever progress in the Wimbledon singles by reaching the final. The speed and muscle and volleys of Althea Gibson, the black American, were too much for her. It was not her first taste of a Wimbledon final. In 1955 she and Anne Shilcock won the ladies' doubles.

When at last Angela gained her singles crown she was an experienced campaigner. The final was her 44th singles. She could also reflect that she was not the first champion to have been born in Plymouth, Devon. The first was May Sutton from California, victor in 1905 and 1907.

Sportingly — for she could have retired with dignity — Angela defended her title in 1962. Her last singles was her loss in the third round to Vera Sukova of Czechoslovakia

After retiring from singles, Angela continued to compete in doubles and mixed doubles for a few years and served as Captain of Britain's Wightman Cup and Federation Cup teams.

**Wimbledon Singles Record:**
1950, played in doubles only.
1951, unseeded, won 0 matches, lost Pat Harrison, 1st round.
1952, unseeded, won 1 match, lost Maureen Connolly, 3rd round.
1953, seeded 5, won 4 matches, lost Dorothy Knode, quarter-final.
1954, seeded 6, won 4 matches, lost Louise Brough, quarter-final.
1955, seeded 4, won 1 match, lost Suzi Kormoczi, 3rd round.
1956, seeded 3, won 4 matches, lost Pat Ward, quarter-final.
1957, seeded 7, won 2 matches, lost Karol Fageros, 3rd round.
1958, unseeded, won 6 matches, lost Althea Gibson, final.
1959, seeded 2, won 3 matches, lost Sandra Reynolds, quarter-final.
1960, seeded 5, won 3 matches, lost Maria Bueno, quarter-final.
1961, seeded 7, won 6 matches, *champion,* (sets 12–1; games 85–47).
1962, seeded 6, won 2 matches, lost Vera Sukova, 3rd round.
1963–1968, played in doubles only.

**Matches:** 36–11; sets 76–28; games 550–327.

**Longest Match:** Quarter-final 1958, beat Margaret du Pont 4–6 6–3 10–8 – a total of 37 games.

**Age on winning singles:** 29 years 78 days.

**Overall Record:**

|  | Titles | Matches | | |
|---|---|---|---|---|
|  |  | Played | Won | Lost |
| Singles | 1 | 47 | 36 | 11 |
| Doubles | 1 | 53 | 35 | 18 |
| Mixed | 0 | 11 | 5 | 6 |
| Total | 2 | 111 | 76 | 35 |

**Career Achievements:**
*The Championships, Wimbledon:* singles 1961; doubles 1955.
*French Championships:* singles 1955.
*Australian Championships:* singles 1958.
*Total Grand Slam titles:* 4 – singles 3, doubles 1.
*German Championships:* doubles 1957.

*Scandinavian Covered Court Championships:* singles 1953–1956, 1959, 1961;
   doubles 1953–1956, 1959–1961; mixed 1954, 1955, 1960, 1961.
*British Hard Court Championships:* singles 1955, 1956, 1959, 1961; doubles 1959,
   1960, 1963.
*British Covered Court Championships:* singles 1952–1954, 1959–1961;
   doubles 1954, 19598, 1961.
*British Wightman Cup team:* 1953, 1955, 1956, 1959–1961, 1964 winning 5 from
   16 matches in 7 ties (singles 3–7; doubles 2–4).

**Full name:** Florence Angela Margaret Mortimer/Barrett
**Born:** 21st April, 1932, Plymouth, Devon, England.
**Married:** John Barrett on 3rd April, 1967, Wimbledon, London, England.

# Karen Susman

1962

## Dynamic and Fragile

Karen Susman, originally Karen Hantze, was, like Maureen Connolly, from San Diego. Like Miss Connolly and like Alice Marble also, she was coached by Teach Tennant. She was the third Wimbledon singles champion to emerge from that remarkable tutorship.

At the age of 11 the tiny Karen was precocious enough to be talked of as a potential champion. Her junior record was exemplary and she was U.S. National Junior Champion at 14. She was ranked 6th in the U.S. at 16.

She made her mark on her first visit to Wimbledon in 1960, winning the international junior singles while also reaching the last eight of the senior event. She was also in the last four of the ladies' doubles with Janet Hopps.

In 1961 she was in harness with Billie Jean Moffitt. They won the doubles with surprising ease. They were not seeded. Miss Moffitt was but 17 and Karen one year older. But Karen could not equal, not surpass, her singles record of the year before.

She was a versatile all court player with a volleying skill that was clearly nurtured in the same stable as Miss Marble. But a blood deficiency left her easily exhausted. To conserve her energies she moved inordinately slowly about the court between rallies. It was not a popular habit.

Her third visit to Wimbledon was as Mrs. Susman in 1962, a year of twofold success for she and Miss Moffitt not only retained their doubles but she was invulnerable in the singles. She was seeded only eighth, the lowest ever to win the title at that time. She had good fortune in that instead of meeting Maria Bueno in the final she clashed with the Czech Vera Sukova who had the ill luck to hurt her ankle on the morning of the match. But Karen yielded a set to no-one at any stage.

She did not defend in 1963 and made no great mark in 1964. Had she possessed more stamina one suspects she would have been more than a one-time singles champion.

**Wimbledon Singles Record:**
1960, unseeded, won 4 matches, lost Christine Truman, quarter-final.
1961, seeded 8, won 4 matches, lost Renee Schuurman, quarter-final.
1962, seeded 8, won 7 matches, *champion,* (sets 14–0; games 93–55).
1963, did not play.
1964, unseeded, won 1 match, lost Margaret Smith, 3rd round.
1965–1976, did not play.
1977, unseeded, won 1 match, lost Helen Sparre-Viragh, 2nd round.

**Matches:** 17–4; sets 36–10; games 268–171.

**Longest Match:** Quarter-final 1960, lost to Christine Truman 4–6 6–4 6–4, and quarter-final 1961, lost to Renee Schuurman 6–4 2–6 7–5 – a total of 30 games.

**Age on winning singles:** 19 years 208 days.

**Overall Record:**

| | Titles | Matches | | |
| --- | --- | --- | --- | --- |
| | | Played | Won | Lost |
| Singles | 1 | 21 | 17 | 4 |
| Doubles | 2 | 21 | 18 | 3 |
| Mixed | 0 | 10 | 7 | 3 |
| Total | 3 | 52 | 42 | 10 |

**Career Achievements:**
*The Championships, Wimbledon:* singles 1962; doubles 1961, 1962.
*U.S. Championships:* doubles 1964.
*Total Grand Slam titles:* 4 – singles 1; doubles 3.
*U.S. Wightman Cup team:* 1960–1962, 1965 winning 6 from 9 matches in 4 ties (singles 3–3; doubles 3–0).
*U.S. Federation Cup team:* 1964, winning 4 from 4 matches in 4 ties (doubles 4–0).

**Full name:** Karen Janice Hantze/Susman
**Born:** 11th December, 1942, San Diego, California, U.S.A.
**Married:** James Susman on 21st September, 1961, San Antonio, Texas, U.S.A.

# Margaret Smith/Court

1963, 1965, 1970

## Champion Extraordinary

Margaret Smith, as she was before marriage, came from a far from affluent family background in Albury on the New South Wales-Victoria border. She was befriended as a junior by Frank Sedgman. Her first coach, who saw her playing on public courts, switched her from being a natural left-hander into right-handed orthodoxy. This she had in common with two other notable champions, Ken Rosewall and Maureen Connolly.

Where she left other champions behind her was in the mass of notable titles she acquired. Between January 1960 (when at the age of 17 she beat Maria Bueno and won the Australian title for the first time) and her eventual retirement in 1977 she achieved every possible tennis feat except one.

She won every event, singles, doubles and mixed, in every Grand Slam title. She achieved the Grand Slam itself in 1970 in singles. She did the same in mixed doubles in 1963. Of the Grand Slam events she won 24 singles, 19 doubles and 19 mixed doubles – that is 62 titles in all. Include other major titles, the Italian, German and South African, and the total of championships comes to 88. It is without equal.

What did she fail to achieve? She was never triple champion at Wimbledon, though she was that in all the other championships I have named. And it needs to be mentioned, I daresay, that she did not win the Grand Slam in ladies' doubles.

Her first big title was, as mentioned, in early 1960. Her last was the ladies' doubles in the U.S. Open in 1975.

Her *forte* was all-round power. Her athleticism was a by-word. She always trained hard and in terms of all-round fitness she was without a peer.

The year 1964 measured her most massive level of achievement. She won 12 major titles and was a triple finalist in Australia, Italy, France and Wimbledon. She won 11 titles in 1965 and was a triple finalist in Australia, France and Germany.

Her principal rivalries were against Maria Bueno and Billie Jean King. Her record against the former was 16–6, against the latter 21–13. Other rivals who were also Wimbledon singles champions were Evonne Cawley, against whom her figures were 16–5. Against Ann Jones she was 9–3. It was 27–3 versus Virginia Wade and 4–2 against Karen Susman. Martina Navratilova was a rival towards the end of her career and against the Czech-born left-hander she was 2–5.

Seeded number two at her first Wimbledon challenge in 1961 the still 18 year old Margaret was spectacularly beaten in the quarter-finals by Britain's heroine Christine Truman. The next year her downfall was even more striking. She was seeded top – for she was currently champion of Australia, Italy and France – but failed to consolidate a winning lead in her first match against Billie Jean Moffitt. From time to time she never quite lived down a reputation as a 'nervy' player who might fail to measure up to her talents.

But in 1963 she broke through Wimbledon's barrier and Miss Moffitt was her victim in the final. She was a triple finalist that year but in doubles won the ladies' and lost the mixed.

1965 brought her a second singles success. It was her most complete victory, for she lost no sets and the only advantage set was in the final against Miss Bueno. The year after she lost in the semi-finals to Billie Jean King, lost in the final of the ladies' doubles and won only the mixed.

In the four years she had taken six titles, played ten finals.

She played nowhere in 1967 but returned to the international arena with the introduction of open tennis in 1968. By then she was Mrs. Barry Court and belonging to Western Australia rather than New South Wales.

Her revival as Wimbledon singles champion came in 1970 and it was a memorable occasion. Seeded one she lost one set in reaching the final, this to Helga Niessen of Germany who paid for her temerity by being worsted in a 6–0 6–0 finish. But if Margaret had had a simple passage, the journey to final success was tempestuous. She played Billie Jean King and probably no more virile contest between women was ever staged. The serve and volley skill shown on both sides was awesome. In the end Margaret won by 14–12 11–9, a total of 46 games and unmatched in its skill and intensity, despite both players carrying an injury.

A dramatic swan song was seemingly performed by Margaret in 1971 when she reached all three finals and met with three defeats. She came back in 1973 as the mother of a baby boy. In the earlier French Championships she had had a notable win against Chris Evert, her victory by 6–7 7–6 6–3 being the outcome of a tremendous duel. On Wimbledon's grass Miss Evert reversed the result at the semi-finals stage. That seemed like a second swan song for the great athlete.

But the actual swan song came in 1975 as, with Marty Riessen, she played and won her last match to climax the meeting, winning the mixed and recording her 10th Wimbledon championship.

She was then a mother. When she retired finally in 1977 – her last tournament was in February in Detroit – it was on the occasion of her third pregnancy. In her career she competed in 289 tournaments and won 383 events in 20 different countries, a remarkable record. In 1991 Margaret was ordained and commenced a life of religious service.

**Wimbledon Singles Record:**
1961, seeded 2, won 3 matches, lost Christine Truman, quarter-final.
1962, seeded 1, won 0 matches, lost Billie Jean Moffitt, 2nd round.
1963, seeded 1, won 6 matches, *champion,* (sets 12–1; games 75–29).
1964, seeded 1, won 5 matches, lost Maria Bueno, final.
1965, seeded 2, won 6 matches, *champion,* (sets 12–0; games 73–21).
1966, seeded 1, won 4 matches, lost Billie Jean King, semi-final.
1967, did not play.
1968, seeded 2, won 3 matches, lost Judy Tegart, quarter-final.
1969, seeded 1, won 4 matches, lost Ann Jones, semi-final.
1970, seeded 1, won 6 matches, *champion,* (sets 12–1; games 91–42).
1971, seeded 1, won 5 matches, lost Evonne Goolagong, final.
1972, did not play.
1973, seeded 1, won 4 matches, lost Chris Evert, semi-final.
1974, did not play.
1975, seeded 5, won 5 matches, lost Evonne Cawley, semi-final.

**Matches:** 51–9; sets 108–28; games 756–379.

**Longest Match:** Final 1970, beat Billie Jean King 14–12 11–9 – a total of 46 games.

**Age on first winning singles:** 20 years 357 days.

**Age on last winning singles:** 27 years 352 days.

**Overall Record:**

| | Titles | Matches Played | Won | Lost |
|---|---|---|---|---|
| Singles | 3 | 60 | 51 | 9 |
| Doubles | 2 | 50 | 41 | 9 |
| Mixed | 5 | 51 | 47 | 4 |
| Total | 10 | 161 | 139 | 22 |

**Career Achievements:**
*The Championships, Wimbledon:* singles 1963, 1965, 1970; doubles 1964, 1969; mixed 1963, 1965, 1966, 1968, 1975.
*U.S. National Championships:* singles 1962, 1965; doubles 1963; mixed 1961, 1962, 1963, 1964, 1965.
*U.S. Open Championships:* singles 1969, 1970, 1973; doubles 1968, 1970, 1973, 1975; mixed 1969, 1970, 1972.
*French Championships:* singles 1962, 1964, 1969, 1970, 1973; doubles 1964, 1965, 1966, 1973; mixed 1963, 1964, 1965, 1969.

*Australian Championships:* singles 1960, 1961, 1962, 1963, 1964, 1965, 1966, 1969, 1970, 1971, 1973; doubles 1961, 1962, 1963, 1965, 1969, 1970, 1971, 1973; mixed 1963, 1964.

*Total Grand Slam titles:* 62 – singles 24, doubles 19, mixed 19.

*Grand Slam:* singles 1970; mixed 1963: (Ken Fletcher)

*Italian Championships:* singles 1962, 1963, 1964, doubles 1963, 1964, 1968; mixed 1961, 1964, 1968.

*German Championships:* singles 1964, 1965, 1966; doubles 1964, 1965, 1966; mixed 1965, 1966.

*South African Championships:* singles 1968, 1970, 1971; doubles 1966, 1971; mixed 1966, 1970, 1971, 1974.

*WTA Tour Championships:* doubles 1973.

*Australian Federation Cup team:* 1963–1965, 1968, 1969, 1971 winning 35 from 40 matches in 20 ties (singles 20–0; doubles 15–5).

*Won:* 92 singles titles, 48 doubles titles (Open Era). Played 649 matches winning 593.

**Full name:** Margaret Smith/Court
**Born:** 16th July, 1942, Albury N.S.W., Australia.
**Married:** Barry Court on 28th October 1967, Perth, Western Australia.

# Billie Jean King

## 1966–1968, 1972, 1973, 1975

## *Championships by the Score*

Billie Jean King, then Billie Jean Moffitt and an ebullient Californian of 17 bubbling with energy, played her first match at Wimbledon in 1961. Her fate was that of most newcomers. She lost her opening singles, this to the Mexican Yola Ramirez. But in doubles her genius was evident. She won with Karen Hantze.

In 1983 Billie Jean played the last match of the meeting. It was the final of the mixed doubles and she and Steve Denton were beaten. It was her 28th final. And, of those 28 finals, she had lost only eight.

The balance, 20 championships – six in the singles, ten in the doubles and four in the mixed – is an awesome record, equalled only by Martina Navratilova in 2003. Her twentieth title was won in 1979, the ladies' doubles with Martina Navratilova. Its achievement had the overtone of a saga, for until Billie Jean equalled it in 1975, Wimbledon's record as the winner of the most titles – 19 – belonged to another Californian, Elizabeth Ryan who had held it since 1934.

The redoubtable Miss Ryan, who had amassed her titles entirely in the ladies' and mixed doubles events, was proud of her record. Then aged 87 she had declared, "I hope I never live to see my record broken". On July 6th, 1979 when, as always, she was an avid spectator, she collapsed at the All England Club and died on the way to hospital still the joint record holder at Wimbledon. On July 7th 1979, less than twenty four hours later, Billie Jean went on court and set the new standard.

At her second visit in 1962 Billie Jean was drawn in her singles opening round against Margaret Smith, then also making her second international tour. Already, though, her reputation was high. The strong, athletic Australian, was the number one seed. It proved a notable clash of two outstanding women volleyers and Billie Jean won 1–6 6–3 7–5. It initiated a decade of memorable rivalry.

Their last Wimbledon meeting was in the final of 1970. By then Billie Jean had already been champion three times and it was her sixth final in that event. Mrs.

Court (as Miss Smith had become) was twice a former winner and in her fourth final. The like of such a battle had not been seen before.

Mrs. Court measured a narrow superiority by 14–12 11–9 after what was arguably the greatest women's match of all time despite the fact that both players were nursing injuries. The sustained vigour and power of the net attack from either side was breath-taking throughout the 46 games, the most ever played in the final. Rarely can victor and vanquished have shared honour so equally.

Billie Jean's first singles title had come in 1966 when she won in three sets in the final against Maria Bueno, her other outstanding rival. A year later she was unbeaten in three events. She was the first triple champion since Frank Sedgman in 1952 and, among women, Doris Hart in 1951.

The first year of the open game, 1968, saw Billie Jean miss the triple crown only when she lost in the semi-finals of the mixed. Up to that stage she had won no less than 30 championship matches without loss. In taking the singles for the third year it meant her last defeat in that event was in the semi-finals in 1965.

Playing her fourth final in as many years Billie Jean yielded the singles in 1969 to Britain's Ann Jones. In 1970, her fifth final in five years, she yielded in her historic clash with Mrs. Court. In 1971 she failed to get beyond the semi-finals for the first time in six years, losing to the now disciplined grace of Evonne Goolagong.

Billie Jean's invincibility was resumed in the next two years. Her 1973 triumph was within the framework of her second triple crown. It gave Billie Jean the singles for the fifth time, the ladies' doubles for the ninth and the mixed for the third.

She won the singles in 1975 (in a sweeping 6–0 6–1 final against Evonne Cawley in 39 minutes) to take the event for the sixth time. It meant that after 15 years she had failed to win a title on only three occasions.

In 1976 her best was to reach the final of the ladies' doubles. It marked 16 years in which she had never failed to play in at least one final. The Centenary Year, 1977, was the first in which she did not play a title match.

In 1981, she did not compete. But in her 40th year, 1983, she was in the singles semi-finals and kept in the mixed as far as the final.

That final (in which John Lloyd and Wendy Turnbull beat Steve Denton and Billie Jean 6–7 7–6 7–5) was Billie Jean's 265th match at Wimbledon. The last set was her 600th. The last game was her 5,670th.

Billie Jean married Larry King, then a student and subsequently a lawyer and sports promoter, in 1965. At her peak it was impossible to find any aspect of her game that was less than strong; her overhead was superb and she was reputed to have gone through more than one season without ever missing a smash.

She played a leading part in lifting the women's professional game towards equality with the men's. She took part in one of the most widely publicised matches of all time, a singles against Bobby Riggs, the 1939 Wimbledon men's champion, in Houston, Texas, on 20th September 1973 that was billed as 'The

Battle of the Sexes'. Billie Jean was 29, Riggs 55. Before a crowd of 30,492 Billie Jean beat Riggs 6–4 6–3 6–3 for a purse of $100,000. In purely lawn tennis terms it meant little. In social terms its impact was unequalled and symbolised the transition of lawn tennis from sport to show business.

**Wimbledon Singles Record:**
1961, unseeded, won 0 matches, lost Yola Ramirez, 2nd round.
1962, unseeded, won 3 matches, lost Ann Haydon, quarter-final.
1963, unseeded, won 5 matches, lost Margaret Smith, final.
1964, seeded 3, won 5 matches, lost Margaret Smith, semi-final.
1965, seeded 5, won 5 matches, lost Maria Bueno, semi-final.
1966, seeded 4, won 7 matches, champion, (sets 14–2, games 96–60).
1967, seeded 1, won 5 matches, champion, (sets 10–0, games 63–28).
1968, seeded 1, won 6 matches, champion, (sets 12–1; games 83–54).
1969, seeded 2, won 5 matches, lost Ann Jones, final.
1970, seeded 2, won 5 matches, lost Margaret Court, final.
1971, seeded 2, won 4 matches, lost Evonne Goolagong, semi-final.
1972, seeded 2, won 6 matches, champion, (sets 12–1, games 75–34).
1973, seeded 2, won 6 matches, champion, (sets 12–2, games 88–50).
1974, seeded 1, won 3 matches, lost Olga Morozova, quarter-final.
1975, seeded 3, won 7 matches, champion, (sets 14–1, games 86–35).
1976, played doubles only.
1977, seeded 5, won 3 matches, lost Chris Evert, quarter-final.
1978, seeded 5, won 4 matches, lost Chris Evert, quarter-final.
1979, seeded 7, won 4 matches, lost Tracy Austin, quarter-final.
1980, seeded 5, won 3 matches, lost Martina Navratilova, quarter-final.
1981, did not play.
1982, seeded 12, won 4 matches, lost Chris Lloyd, semi-final.
1983, seeded 10, won 5 matches, lost Andrea Jaeger, semi-final.

**Matches:** 95–15; sets 198–53; games 1437–928.

**Longest match:** Final 1970 lost to Margaret Court 14–12 11–9 – a total of 46 games.

**Age on first winning singles:** 22 years 222 days.

**Age on last winning singles:** 31 years 224 days.

**Overall Record:**

|  | Titles | Matches Played | Won | Lost |
|---|---|---|---|---|
| Singles | 6 | 110 | 95 | 15 |
| Doubles | 10 | 86 | 74 | 12 |
| Mixed | 4 | 69 | 55 | 14 |
| Total | 20 | 265 | 224 | 41 |

**Career Achievements:**

*The Championships, Wimbledon:* singles 1966, 1967, 1968, 1972, 1973, 1975; doubles 1961, 1962, 1965, 1967, 1968, 1970, 1971, 1972, 1973, 1979; mixed 1967, 1971, 1973, 1974.

*U.S. Championships:* singles 1967, 1971, 1972, 1974; doubles 1964, 1967, 1974, 1978, 1980; mixed 1967, 1971, 1973, 1976.

*French Championships:* singles 1972; doubles 1972; mixed 1967, 1970.

*Australian Championships:* singles 1968; mixed 1968.

*Total Grand Slam titles:* 39-singles 12, doubles 16, mixed 11.

*Italian Championships:* singles 1970; doubles 1970.

*German Championships:* singles 1971; doubles 1971.

*South African Championships:* singles 1966, 1967, 1969; doubles 1967, 1970: mixed 1967.

*U.S. Wightman Cup team:* 1961–1967, 1970, 1977, 1978, winning 21 from 26 matches in 10 ties (singles 14–2; doubles 7–3).

*U.S. Federation Cup team:* 1963, 1967, 1976–1979, winning 52 from 58 matches in 36 ties (singles 25–4; doubles 27–1, with one unfinished).

*Won:* 67 singles titles, 101 doubles titles (Open Era). Played 850 singles matches winning 695.

*Prize money:* $1,966,478.

**Full name:** Billie Jean Moffitt/King.
**Born:** 22nd November, 1943, Long Beach, California, U.S.A.
**Married:** L.W. King on 17th September, 1965, Long Beach, California, U.S.A.

# Ann Jones

## 1969

## Craft and Diligence

Ann Jones won the singles in 1969 at the age of 30 when competing for the 14th successive year and did not play again in singles. At that time no player had had to be so diligent before succeeding. She was also the first left-handed woman to win. She was only the fourth British woman to triumph in the singles since World War I (the others were Kitty Godfree, Dorothy Round and Angela Mortimer).

She was born Adrianne Shirley Haydon, in Birmingham on 7th October, 1938. Both her parents were notable table tennis players and it was at that sport she first excelled. In various events she was five times a finalist for a World Championship without ever winning one.

At lawn tennis she became British Junior Champion in 1954 and 1955. Then, as throughout her career, she was an astute tactician of patience, albeit with no small measure of volleying skill. Her loyalty to all levels of the game was marked. After giving up as an active professional she took a leading part in the administration of the women's game, serving as one of the International Tennis Federation members on the Women's International Professional Tennis Council and acting as Referee at the pre-Wimbledon Eastbourne event. At a more modest level she was conspicuous as an assiduous member of the Warwickshire County side and in representative matches for her club, Edgbaston-Priory.

She married Mr. Philip 'Pip' Jones, formerly a business man, in 1962. They had three children.

Her eventual Wimbledon triumph was the outcome of a remarkable *tour-de-force* in the last two rounds. In the semi-finals she beat Margaret Court, the number one seed, 10–12 6–3 6–2. In the final she beat Billie Jean King, the second seed, 3–6 6–3 6–2, despite four earlier losses to her at Wimbledon. This glorious performance was capped by winning the mixed doubles title with the Australian Fred Stolle. She was the losing finalist in that event with Dennis Ralston in 1962 and in 1968 she had also been a final loser with Françoise Durr. Mrs. King was her victor in the singles final of 1967. Including her two successes Ann played five Wimbledon finals in all.

## Wimbledon Singles Record:

1956, unseeded, won 1 match, lost Anne Shilcock, 2nd round.

1957, unseeded, won 1 match, lost Edda Buding, 3rd round.

1958, unseed, won 5 matches, lost Althea Gibson, semi-final.

1959, seeded 8, won 4 matches, lost Darlene Hard, quarter-final.

1960, seeded 4, won 5 matches, lost Sandra Reynolds, semi-final.

1961, seeded 3, won 3 matches, lost Renee Schuurman, 3rd round.

1962, seeded 5, won 4 matches, lost Karen Susman, semi-final.

1963, seeded 3, won 5 matches, lost Billie Jean Moffitt, semi-final.

1964, seeded 6, won 4 matches, lost Billie Jean Moffitt, quarter-final.

1965, unseeded, won 2 matches, lost Maria Bueno, 4th round.

1966, seeded 3, won 5 matches, lost Maria Bueno, semi-final.

1967, seeded 3, won 6 matches, lost Billie Jean King, final.

1968, seeded 4, won 5 matches, lost Billie Jean King, semi-final.

1969, seeded 4, won 7 matches, champion, (sets 14–2; games 101–47).

1977, played doubles only.

**Matches:** 57–13; sets 121–37; games 879–502.

**Longest Match:** Semi-final 1966, lost to Maria Bueno 6–3 9–11 7–5 – a total of 41 games.

**Age on winning singles:** 30 years 270 days.

### Overall Record:

| | Titles | Matches Played | Won | Lost |
|---|---|---|---|---|
| Singles | 1 | 70 | 57 | 13 |
| Doubles | 0 | 48 | 33 | 15 |
| Mixed | 1 | 39 | 29 | 10 |
| Total | 2 | 157 | 119 | 38 |

### Career Achievements:

*The Championships, Wimbledon:* singles 1969; mixed 1969.

*French Championships:* singles 1961, 1966; doubles 1963, 1968, 1969.

*Total Grand Slam titles:* 7 – singles 3, doubles 3, mixed 1.

*Italian Championships:* singles 1966; doubles 1969.

*British Federation Cup team:* 1963–1967, 1971, winning 21 from 33 matches in 18 ties (singles 10–7; doubles 11–5 with one unfinished).

*British Wightman Cup team:* 1957–1967, 1970, 1975, winning 16 from 32 matches in 13 ties (singles 10–11; doubles 6–5).

**Full name:** Adrianne Shirley Haydon/Jones

**Born:** 7th October, 1938, Birmingham, England.

**Married:** Philip Jones on 30th August 1962, Hampstead, London, England.

# Evonne Goolagong/Cawley

## 1971, 1980

### The Joy Maker

Few champions have given so much pleasure to spectators as Evonne Cawley. She came first to Europe in 1970 as Evonne Goolagong at the age of 18 already well known, not only for her high promise but because she was of a racial mix never before seen in lawn tennis. She was part aborigine. She had been coached and looked after for some years by the well know Australian coach Vic Edwards.

Evonne's brilliance on the court was obvious from the first, for she was an unusually fine touch player, albeit with a forehand that was suspect. But her endearing quality was her apparent joy in playing. She radiated fun and reminded one of the real values of lawn tennis in that it was a game to be enjoyed.

So great an attraction was she from the first that there was little choice but to stage her second match at Wimbledon on the Centre Court. Few newcomers can have had so gruelling an initiation and Evonne paid the penalty, losing to the ultra steady American Peaches Bartkowicz.

A year later, when she was 19, her genius flowered richly. She won the French Championship in Paris and came on to Wimbledon and conquered there from her position as the third seed. She beat Billie Jean King in the semi-finals, her compatriot Margaret Court in the final, each in two sets. No champion could have been more convincing.

Evonne was a threat for the next five years but a doubles win in 1974 was her only reward. Three times she lost in the final. She almost gave the impression that she was too nice to win.

In 1975 she married the Britisher Roger Cawley, who came from Kent. The idyll of the romance was marred somewhat since it brought a break with Vic Edwards who, apart from being her coach, was virtually an adoptive father.

The birth of her first child prevented her challenge in 1977. She was in the van again for the next two years. Then in 1980, nine years away from her first success, she stole the singles once more, ruggedly surviving the loss of three sets in the course of it. She was the first mother to win since 1914.

**Wimbledon Singles Record:**

1970, unseeded, won 1 match, lost Jane Bartkowicz, 2nd round.

1971, seeded 3, won 7 matches, champion, (sets 14–1; games 85–40).

1972, seeded 1, won 5 matches, lost Billie Jean King, final.

1973, seeded 3, won 5 matches, lost Billie Jean King, semi-final.

1974, seeded 3, won 4 matches, lost Kerry Melville, quarter-final.

1975, seeded 4, won 5 matches, lost Billie Jean King, final.

1976, seeded 2, won 6 matches, lost Chris Evert, final.

1977, did not play.

1978, seeded 3, won 4 matches, lost Martinia Navratilova, semi-final.
1979, seeded 3, won 5 matches, lost Chris Lloyd, semi-final.
1980, seeded 4, won 7 matches, champion, (sets 14–3; games 94–54).
1981, did not play.
1982, seeded 16, won 0 matches, lost Zena Garrison, 1st round.
1983, played doubles only.

**Matches:** 49–9; sets 102–28; games 719–442.

**Longest Match:** Quarter-final 1975, beat Virginia Wade 5–7 6–3 9–7 – a total of 37 games.

**Age on first winning singles:** 19 years 336 days.

**Age on last winning singles:** 28 years 339 days.

**Overall Record:**

| | | Matches | | |
| --- | --- | --- | --- | --- |
| | *Titles* | *Played* | *Won* | *Lost* |
| Singles | 2 | 58 | 49 | 9 |
| Doubles | 1 | 28 | 21 | 7 |
| Mixed | 0 | 27 | 19 | 8 |
| Total | 3 | 113 | 89 | 24 |

**Career Achievements:**
*The Championships, Wimbledon:* singles 1971, 1980; doubles 1974.
*French Championships:* singles 1971; mixed 1972.
*Australian Championships:* singles 1974, 1975, 1976, 1978; doubles 1971, 1974, 1975, 1976.
*Total Grand Slam titles:* 13: singles 7; doubles 5; mixed 1.
*Italian Championships:* singles 1973.
*South African Championships:* singles 1972; doubles 1971, 1972.
*WTA Tour Championships:* singles 1974, 1976.
*Australian Federation Cup team:* 1971–1976, 1982 winning 35 from 40 matches in 26 ties (singles 22–3; doubles 13–2).
*Won:* 68 singles titles, 11 doubles titles.
*Played:* 853 singles, winning 695.
*Prize money:* $1,399,431.

**Full name:** Evonne Fay Goolagong/Cawley
**Born:** 31st July, 1951, Barellan, N.S.W., Australia.
**Married:** Roger Cawley on 19th June, 1975, Canterbury, Kent, England.

# Chris Evert/Lloyd

1974, 1976, 1981

## *Little Miss America*

Chris Evert, born at Fort Lauderdale in Florida, made a dramatic start in the international game in 1970 when, aged only 15, she beat the current Wimbledon champion, Margaret Court, in the semi-finals of a tournament in Charlotte, North Carolina. She won 7–6 7–6.

Nearly a year later this determined young lady, who had been prepared for stardom by her father Jimmy, the teaching professional at Holiday Park in Fort Lauderdale, threw down the gauntlet into the adult international arena with an emphasis that was equally striking. In the annual Wightman Cup tie against Great Britain in Cleveland, Ohio, playing the opening rubber in her novice effort at 16, she beat Winnie Shaw. On the third day she also beat Virginia Wade, in both cases with authority.

A week or two later Chris played for the first time in the US Open Championships. She survived six match points in a quarter-final against Lesley Hunt of Australia before losing her semi-final to Billie Jean King. A long record of rare consistency had that match, played in September 1971, as its starting point. It came to an end when she finally retired after losing to Zina Garrison in the quarter-finals of the 1989 US Open. It was her 114th match at her 19th national Championships where she had made herself the champion on six occasions.

During that spell of eighteen years the consummate steadiness and shrewd courtcraft, together with a double-fisted backhand that her own example had made commonplace among the new generation, brought massive success. She prospered at the other three Grand Slams as she did at home winning the French singles title seven times (a record), the Wimbledon singles thrice and the Australian twice.

In her challenge for 56 Grand Slam singles titles she failed on only four occasions to reach at least the semi-final stage, a prodigious record. The one time at Wimbledon was in 1983 when she fell to Kathy Jordan in the third round.

Chris' three Championships at Wimbledon occurred in 1974, 1976 and 1981 when she defeated in the final Olga Morozova, Evonne Cawley and Hana Mandlikova respectively. Apart from these occasions, Chris contested seven other singles finals losing to King and Cawley once each and to Martina Navratilova five times, all in the eighties, when Miss Navratilova was at her peak. Only in the early years of 1976 and 1980 was Chris able to master her rival on grass.

Ball control and command of length were the classic ingredients of Chris' mastery. If best on the slow rubble of what used to be called hard courts in Britain and clay in the USA , she was equally a champion on any surface. Her consistency was measured by a winning sequence of 125 matches on clay, beginning at the US Clay Court Championships in Indianapolis in August 1973 and ending with her loss to Tracy Austin in the semi-finals of the Italian Championships in 1979.

In all she captured 154 singles titles, 18 of them Grand Slams, and eight in doubles from 289 events and won 1,309 matches. From 1972 to 1989 she never appeared in the world ranking lists lower than No. 4 and for a total of 262 weeks held the No. 1 position, ending the year atop the rankings on five occasions.

In 1976 Chris became the first woman player to win one million dollars in prize money and upon retirement that total had risen to $8,896,195.

In team events Chris excelled. She played in the Wightman Cup for 13 years, attaining a 26–0 record in singles and in the Federation Cup her singles record between 1977 and 1989 was 40 wins and just two losses. There was another con-

tribution to American teams from the Evert family. Chris' sister Jeanne played for the US in the Wightman Cup teams of 1973 and 1974.

In 1979 Chris married the British Davis Cup player John Lloyd, but they divorced amicably in 1987. A year later she married the Olympic skier, Andy Mill and they had three sons – Alexander, Nicholas and Colton.

**Wimbledon Singles Record:**

1972, seeded 4, won 5 matches, lost Evonne Goolagong, semi-final.

1973, seeded 4, won 6 matches, lost Billie Jean King, final.

1974, seeded 2, won 6 matches champion (sets 12–1; games 85–45).

1975, seeded 1, won 5 matches, lost Bille Jean King, semi-final.

1976, seeded 1, won 7 matches, champion (sets 14–2; games 94–39).

1977, seeded 1, won 5 matches, lost Virginia Wade, semi-final.

1978, seeded 1, won 5 matches, lost Martina Navratilova, final.

1979, seeded 2, won 6 matches, lost Martina Navratilova, final.

1980, seeded 3, won 5 matches, lost Evonne Cawley, final.

1981, seeded 1, won 7 matches, champion, (sets 14–0; games 85–26).

1982, seeded 2, won 5 matches, lost Martina Navratilova, final.

1983, seeded 2, won 2 matches, lost Kathy Jordan, 3rd round.

1984, seeded 2, won 6 matches, lost Martina Navratilova, final.

1985, seeded 1, won 6 matches, lost Martina Navratilova, final.

1986, seeded 2, won 5 matches, lost Hana Mandlikova, semi-final.

1987, seeded 3, won 5 matches, lost Martina Navratilova, semi-final.

1988, seeded 4, won 5 matches, lost Martina Navratilova, semi-final.

1989, seeded 4, won 5 matches, lost Steffi Graf, semi-final.

**Matches:** 96–15; sets 200–51; games 1400–779.

**Longest Match:** 1st Round in 1974, beat Lesley Hunt 8–6 5–7 11–9 – a total of 46 games.

**Age on first winning singles:** 19 years 196 days.

**Age on last winning singles:** 26 years 194 days.

**Overall Record:**

| | Titles | Matches | | |
| --- | --- | --- | --- | --- |
| | | Played | Won | Lost |
| Singles | 3 | 111 | 96 | 15 |
| Doubles | 1 | 52 | 37 | 15 |
| Mixed | 0 | 11 | 7 | 4 |
| Total | 4 | 174 | 140 | 34 |

**Career Achievements:**

*The Championships, Wimbledon:* singles 1974, 1976, 1981; doubles 1976.

*U.S. Championships:* singles 1975, 1976, 1977, 1978, 1980, 1982.

*French Championships:* singles 1974, 1975, 1979, 1980, 1983, 1985, 1986; doubles 1974, 1975.

*Australian Championships:* singles 1982, 1984.

*Total Grand Slam titles:* 21 – singles 18; doubles 3.

*Italian Championships:* singles 1974, 1975, 1980, 1981, 1982; doubles 1974, 1975.

*German Championships:* singles 1983.

*South African Championships:* singles 1973.

*WTA Tour Championships:* singles 1972, 1973, 1975, 1977

*U.S. Federation Cup team:* 1977_1982, 1986, 1987, 1989, winning 57 from 61 matches in 40 ties (singles 40-2, doubles 17-2).

*U.S. Wightman Cup team:* 1971–1973, 1975–1982, 1984, 1985 winning 34 from 38 matches in 13 ties (singles 26–0, doubles 8–4).

*Won:* 154 singles titles, 8 doubles titles.

*Played:* 1455 singles matches, winning 1309.

*Prize money:* $8,896,195

**Full name:** Christine Marie Evert/Lloyd/Mill

**Born:** 21st December 1954 at Fort Lauderdale, Florida, U.S.A.

**Married:** John Lloyd on 17th April 1979, Fort Lauderdale, Florida, U.S.A.
Andy Mill on 30th July, 1988, Miami, Florida, U.S.A.

# Virginia Wade

## 1977

### The Centenary Champion

Virginia Wade won the singles in 1977 and no British player could have timed her inspiration better. It was the year of Wimbledon's Centenary Celebrations and the Silver Jubilee of Queen Elizabeth II. Her Majesty was in the Royal Box on Friday 1st July to see Virginia beat Betty Stove of The Netherlands in three untidy but patriotically sparkling sets.

Thus did Virginia crown a long and valiant effort. Nine days later she celebrated her 32nd birthday. It was her 16th challenge at Wimbledon and her best had been a semi-finals appearance the year before and two years before that. The key to her victory was a doughty win at that stage over the holder Chris Evert.

If consistency of effort were a characteristic of Virginia, consistency of performance was not. No-one was more aggressive, more ready to volley. Her service could be deadly. But when accuracy of shot eluded her she beat herself. Her career was marked by peaks and troughs. The first peak was when she won the first U.S. Open singles at Forest Hills in 1968. She took the Italian singles in 1971, the Australian in 1972. But no other player in history, man or woman, had waited so long to take a Wimbledon title.

Virginia was born in Bournemouth. Her formative years, until she was 15, were in South Africa, where her father was Archdeacon of Durban. As a student at Sussex University she brought off the remarkable achievement in 1966 of playing for Britain in the Wightman Cup at Wimbledon while sitting her finals for her degree – and getting a science degree that was adequate if not brilliant in its class.

Virginia continued to compete in the singles at Wimbledon up to 1985 when she registered her 24th consecutive year – an all time record. She never failed to participate in the Wightman Cup from 1965 to 1985 and in Zurich in 1983 she played her 100th rubber in the Federation Cup.

At that time she had made lawn tennis history by being the first woman to be elected to the Wimbledon Championships Committee. No British player, man or woman, has played so much or won so many matches as Virginia at the tournament.

## Wimbledon Singles Record:

1962, unseeded, won 1 match, lost Judy Tegart, 2nd round.

1963, unseeded, won 1 match, lost Ann Jones, 2nd round.

1964, unseeded, won 1 match lost Judy Alvarez, 2nd round.

1965, unseeded, won 2 matches, lost Justina Bricka, 4th round.

1966, unseeded, won 0 matches, lost Judy Tegart, 2nd round.

1967, seeded 8, won 3 matches, lost Billie Jean King, quarter-final.

1968, seeded 5, won 0 matches, lost Christine Sandberg, 1st round.

1969, seeded 3, won 2 matches, lost Pat Walkden, 3rd round.

1970, seeded 3, won 3 matches, lost Ceci Marinez, 4th round.

1971, seeded 5, won 3 matches, lost Judy Dalton, 4th round.

1972, seeded 7, won 3 matches, lost Billie Jean King, quarter-final.

1973, seeded 6, won 4 matches, lost Evonne Goolagong, quarter-final.

1974, seeded 5, won 5 matches, lost Olga Morozova, semi-final.

1975, seeded 6, won 3 matches, lost Evonne Cawley, quarter-final.

1976, seeded 3, won 5 matches, lost Evonne Cawley, semi-final.

1977, seeded 3, won 7 matches, champion, (sets 14–2; games 96–46).

1978, seeded 4, won 5 matches, lost Chris Evert semi-final.

1979, seeded 5, won 4 matches, lost Evonne Cawley, quarter-final.
1980, seeded 7, won 3 matches, lost Andrea Jaeger, 4th round.
1981, unseeded, won 0 matches, lost Ann Hobbs, 2nd round.
1982, unseeded, won 1 match, lost Marjorie Blackwood, 2nd round.
1983, unseeded, won 4 matches, lost Yvonne Vermaak, quarter-final.
1984, unseeded, won 2 matches, lost Carina Karlsson, 3rd round.
1985, unseeded, won 2 matches, lost Pam Shriver, 3rd round.
1986, played doubles only.
1987, played doubles only.

**Matches:** 64–23; sets 137–64; games 1095–831.

**Longest Match:** 2nd round 1964, lost to Judy Alvarez 7–9 6–3 8–6 – a total of 39 games.

**Age on winning singles:** 31 years 356 days.

**Overall Record:**

|  | Titles | Matches | | |
|---|---|---|---|---|
|  |  | Played | Won | Lost |
| Singles | 1 | 87 | 64 | 23 |
| Doubles | 0 | 77 | 53 | 24 |
| Mixed | 0 | 48 | 24 | 24 |
| Total | 1 | 212 | 141 | 71 |

**Career Achievements:**
*The Championships, Wimbledon:* singles, 1977.
*U.S. Championships:* singles 1968; doubles 1973, 1975.
*French Championships:* doubles 1973.
*Australian Championships:* singles 1972; doubles 1973.
*Total Grand Slam titles:* 7–singles 3, doubles 4.
*Italian Championships:* singles 1971; doubles 1968, 1971, 1973.
*British Federation Cup team:* 1967–1983, winning 66 from 99 matches (36 from 56 singles; 30 from 43 doubles with one unfinished) in 57 ties.
*British Wightman Cup team:* 1965–1985 winning 19 from 56 matches (12 from 35 singles: 7 from 21 doubles) in 21 ties.
*Won:* 55 titles.
*Prize money:* $1,542,278.

**Full name:** Sarah Virginia Wade
**Born:** 10th July, 1945, Bournemouth, Hampshire, England.

# Martina Navratilova

1978, 1979, 1982–1987, 1990

## *Record Breaker Extraordinary*

The Bohemian tradition of high lawn tennis standards goes back a long way. Before the first World War they looked like swamping the entry for the 1908 Olympics at Wimbledon, though in the event few actually competed. Since World War ll Jaroslav Drobny, Jan Kodes and Ivan Lendl made themselves champions at the Grand Slam level.

The standard of women's play was taken to its highest level ever by Martina Navratilova, a brave left-handed volleyer whose 350 career titles – 167 in singles, 174 in doubles and 9 in mixed – make her the most successful tennis player of all time, male or female. Seven times she ended the year as the world's top ranked player (one less than Steffi Graf) and altogether spent 331 weeks atop the computer rankings. Her prize money of over $21 million also made her the richest female athlete in history until overtaken by Graf at the end of her career.

If Martina's greatest exploits were achieved as an American it cannot be gainsaid that her roots and training were entirely Czech. She had recognition first in 1973 when, aged 16, she was the leading member of the Czech side that won the BP Cup in Torquay early in the year. A few months later she competed at Wimbledon for the first time.

In 1975 she led Czechoslovakia to victory in the Federation Cup at Aix-En-Provence. In the autumn of that year, during the course of the US Open, she asked for refugee status in America, a bold decision for a girl still not yet 19 years old who would effectively be cutting herself off permanently from family and friends in Prague.

Her earliest efforts on the professional circuit in the US were sometimes not in keeping with her obvious talent. Martina succumbed to the temptations of rich American food and put on weight. Later she learned to discipline her eating habits and adopted the Haas diet. With the help of various experts she also began to train more rigorously.

Martina acquired her first Wimbledon title in 1976 with Chris Evert in the doubles, an event she later took with Billie Jean King and, five times, with Pam Shriver. Her breakthrough as singles champion was in 1978 when she survived a hard buffeting and won the final against the same Miss Evert. This was the first of Martina's record-breaking nine singles titles and the first of five winning finals against her great American friend and rival. How unlucky for both that their careers overlapped, but what excitement and spectacle they provided for tennis fans around the world as they battled for supremacy. They met on 80 occasions altogether with Martina winning 43 of those encounters.

By the time of her third success against Evert (now Mrs. John Lloyd) in 1982, Martina was an American citizen. She had been naturalized on 21st July the previous year. In 1983 Martina had her most successful Championship thus far, winning the singles without losing a set, a feat she would repeat the following year and twice more – in 1986 and 1990. Martina achieved as much in doubles, too, during her fifth and last success with Pam Shriver in 1986.

As her career unfolded with success in all the major Championships, even in Paris where her 6–3 6–1 over clay-court expert Evert in 1984 displayed her aggressive talents in all their glory, there was a feeling that we were witnessing the progress of the greatest champion of all time. Yet still Martina had not equalled

Billie Jean King's Wimbledon record of 20 titles. When she arrived in the 1994 final to face Conchita Martinez of Spain there was a chance of capturing a 19th for the previous year she had improved her total to 18 by making herself the mixed doubles champion with Australia's Mark Woodforde.

Martinez, though, was intent on claiming her own moment of glory. Hitting her backhand passing shots with unerring precision she blunted Martina's attack and beat her 6–4 3–6 6–3. The Centre Court crowd could hardly believe what they had witnessed. As Martina left the arena she turned, bent down to pluck some blades of grass from the court and smiled bravely as she waved farewell to her legion of applauding fans.

Announcing afterwards that she had played her last singles match, Martina seemed destined never to catch Billie Jean King. Yet hope was rekindled the following year when she teamed with compatriot Jonathan Stark to claim a 19th title.

There followed a period when Martina had virtually retired. Not until 2002 did she win another title, that the doubles in Madrid with Natasha Zvereva. Saying that she was enjoying the return to competition Martina got herself back to full fitness for 2003 and started collecting doubles titles at an alarming rate. Seven would fall to her that year, five of them with the 18–year-old Russian Svetlana Kuznetsova, a triumph for a woman in her 47th year. But the greatest triumph of all came at Wimbledon. Teaming in mixed with the effervescent Indian Leander Paes, Martina rode an emotional wave all the way to her 20th title to equal the record and be the oldest player, man or woman, to win a Wimbledon title, at 46 years 261 days. The scenes on Centre Court as she hugged her partner were unforgettable. It was an appropriate postscript to a glorious career.

Yet it was not a postscript after all. Many of Martina's fans were sad to learn that the great champion had asked for a wild card in singles for the 2004 Championships. It was obvious that she would be beaten early. Having won her opening round against a clearly terrified Catalina Castano of Colombia, Martina was duly dismissed by Argentina's Gisela Dulko. Most will want to forget that ignominious exit and remember the good times. They were spectacular indeed.

**Wimbledon Singles Record:**
1973, unseeded, won 2 matches, lost Pattti Hogan, 3rd round.
1974, unseeded, won 0 matches, lost Mima Jausovec, 1st round.
1975, seeded 2, won 4 matches, lost Margaret Court, quarter-final.
1976, seeded 4, won 5 matches, lost Chris Evert, semi-final.
1977, seeded 2, won 4 matches, lost Betty Stove, quarter-final.
1978, seeded 2, won 7 matches, champion, (sets 14–3, games 93–61).
1979, seeded 1, won 7 matches, champion, (sets 14–3, games 98–59).
1980, seeded 1, won 5 matches, lost Chris Evert, semi-final.
1981, seeded 4, won 5 matches, lost Hana Mandlikova, semi-final.
1982, seeded 1, won 6 matches, champion, (sets 12–1, games 75–36).

1983, seeded 1, won 7 matches, champion, (sets 14–0, games 85–25).
1984, seeded 1, won 7 matches, champion, (sets 13–0, games 80–35).
1985, seeded 1, won 7 matches, champion, (sets 14–1, games 91–50).
1986, seeded 1, won 7 matches, champion, (sets 14–0, games 85–34).
1987, seeded 1, won 7 matches, champion, (sets 14–1, games 90–36).
1988, seeded 2, won 6 matches, lost Steffi Graf, final.
1989, seeded 2, won 6 matches, lost Steffi Graf, final.
1990, seeded 2, won 7 matches, champion, (sets 14–0, games 84–29).
1991, seeded 3, won 4 matches, lost Jennifer Capriati, quarter-final.
1992, seeded 4, won 5 matches, lost Monica Seles, semi-final.
1993, seeded 2, won 5 matches, lost Jana Novotna, semi-final.
1994, seeded 4, won 6 matches, lost Conchita Martinez, final.
1995–1996, played doubles only.

1997–1999, did not play.
2000–2003, played doubles only.
2004, unseeded, won 1 match, lost to Gisela Dulko, 2nd round.

**Matches:** 120–14; 249–49; 1687–928

**Longest match:** Quarter-final 1980, beat Billie Jean King 7–6, 1–6, 10–8 – a total of 38 games.

**Age on first winning singles:** 21 years 262 days.

**Age on last winning singles:** 33 years 262 days.

**Overall Record:**

|  | Titles | Matches Played | Won | Lost |
|---|---|---|---|---|
| Singles | 9 | 134 | 120 | 14 |
| Doubles | 7 | 112 | 93 | 19 |
| Mixed | 4 | 67 | 53 | 13 |
| Total | 20 | 312 | 266 | 46 |

**Career Achievements:**

*The Championships, Wimbledon:* singles 1978, 1979, 1982, 1983, 1984, 1985, 1986, 1987, 1990: doubles 1976, 1979, 1981, 1982, 1983, 1984, 1986: mixed 1985, 1993, 1995, 2003.

*U.S. Championships:* singles 1983, 1984, 1986, 1987: doubles 1977, 1978, 1980, 1983, 1984,1986, 1987, 1989, 1990: mixed 1985, 1987.

*French Championships:* singles 1982, 1984: doubles 1975, 1982, 1984, 1985, 1986, 1987, 1988: mixed 1974, 1985.

*Australian Championships:* singles 1981, 1983, 1985: doubles 1980, 1982, 1983, 1984, 1985,1987, 1988, 1989: mixed 2003.

*Total Grand Slam titles:* 58 – singles 18, doubles 31, mixed 9.

*Grand Slam doubles:* 1984 (Pam Shriver)

*Italian Championships:* doubles 1975, 1987, 2003.

*WTA Tour Championships:* singles 1978, 1979, 1981 1983, 1984, 1985, 1986 (Mar.), 1986 (Nov.) doubles 1980–1985, 1986 (Nov.) – 1989, 1991.

*Czechoslovakian Federation Cup team:* 1975, winning 9 from 9 matches in 5 ties (singles 5–0, doubles 4–0)

*U.S. Federation/Fed Cup team:* 1982, 1986, 1989, 1995, 2003, 2004, winning 31 from 32 matches in 20 ties (singles 15–0, doubles 16–11).

*U.S. Wightman Cup team:* 1983, winning 3 from 3 matches (singles 2–0, doubles 1–0).

*Won:* 167 singles titles and 174 doubles and 9 mixed titles.

*Played:* 1653 singles matches, winning 1440.

*Prize money:* $21,194,804.

**Full name:** Martina Navratilova
**Born:** 18th October, 1956, Prague, Czechoslovakia.

# Steffi Graf

1988, 1989, 1991–1993,
1995, 1996

## *Golden Grand Slam Champion*

Steffi Graf arrived at Wimbledon in 1984 shortly after her 15th birthday. The quiet, long-limbed young German was already a fine athlete with the build of a long distance runner and a forehand that was lethal.

Fifteen years later she appeared on Centre Court for the last time in her ninth singles final, now established as the greatest woman player of her generation, arguably the greatest of all time.

With a total of 22 Grand Slam singles titles to her name, Steffi was only two short of Margaret Court's record total of major wins but the great Australian's haul had included 11 national titles in an era when few overseas women ventured down under.

In terms of world rankings and prize money Steffi was without equal. Eight times she was the year-end world No.1 and altogether she amassed $21,895,277 in on-court earnings, both all-time records.

Graf's *annus mirabilis* was 1988. Her Grand Slam that year equalled the feats of Maureen Connolly (1953) and Margaret Court (1970) but with tennis newly restored to the Olympic Games as a full medal sport Graf had the chance to make history. She took it brilliantly in Seoul by winning the gold medal to crown a year of achievement that may never be equalled.

Born at Neckarau, near Mannheim, in Southern Germany, not far from Boris Becker's birthplace of Leimen, Steffi was coached by her father Peter from an early age. At first she used a squash racket with a sawn off handle until she was strong enough to play with a junior tennis racket. In due course she became the European 12–and-under champion and would repeat that feat at the 18 and under level. In between those victories Steffi, aged 13 years four months, became the second youngest player ever to earn a ranking on the women's Tour (Stephanie Rehe was the youngest at 13.1 in 1982).

When Steffi entered the women's circuit in 1982 Peter realized she needed a regular hitting partner and engaged the former touring player Pavel Slozil of Czechoslovakia to fill that role. To see the two of them on the practice court was to marvel at Steffi's uninhibited baseline aggression and her speed about the court. Without the pressure of a match Steffi was also able to hit flat or topspin backhands, a shot that was never fully integrated into her match repertoire.

Steffi worked with Slozil until 1990 when Heinz Guenthardt, the former Swiss No.1, took over the coaching duties until Steffi's retirement from the game in August 1999.

What, then, were the qualities that set Graf apart? She had exceptional speed of foot, a penetrating sliced backhand that was used to set up chances for her winning forehand and a first class serve. Nor was Steffi a bad volleyer, but so dominant was she from the baseline that it was seldom necessary to advance to the net to win a point.

A born competitor, Steffi had a ruthless will to win and was also blessed with exceptional powers of concentration. After overtaking Martina as the No.1 player in the world in August 1987 Steffi began to accumulate all sorts of records. Altogether she would reign atop the computer ranking list for a total of 377 weeks, 186 of them consecutively – both world records. Her capture of the 1995 US Open meant that she had now won each of the four Grand Slam titles at least four times, another record which may never be broken.

Steffi's run of seven Wimbledon wins in nine years began in 1988 with the first of two successive victories over Navratilova, a win that reversed the result of the previous year's final. That same year Steffi won her only Grand Slam doubles title at Wimbledon in partnership with the popular Argentine, Gabriela Sabatini.

Her only other loss in a singles final came in 1999 when the powerful American Lindsay Davenport set the game off on a period of success for the power merchants. In between Steffi repulsed challenges from Gabriela Sabatini ('91), Monica Seles ('92), Jana Novotna ('93) and Arantxa Sanchez-Vicario ('95 and '96).

Always a very private person Steffi took the world by surprise when she married Andre Agassi in October 2001. They have two children, a son Jaden Gill born in 2001 and a daughter, Jaz, born two years later.

**Wimbledon Singles Record:**
1984, unseeded, won 3 matches, lost Jo Durie, 4th round.
1985, seeded No. 11, won 3 matches, lost Pam Shriver, 4th round.
1986, did not play.
1987, seeded No. 2, won 6 matches, lost Martina Navratilova, final.
1988, seeded No. 1, won 7 matches, champion, (Sets 14–1, games 89–27).
1989, seeded No. 1, won 7 matches, champion, (Sets 14–1, games 91–30).
1990, seeded No. 1, won 5 matches, lost Zina Garrison, semi-final.
1991, seeded No. 1, won 7 matches, champion, (Sets 14–2, games 89–39).
1992, seeded No. 2, won 7 matches, champion, (Sets 14–2, games 94–39).
1993, seeded No. 1, won 7 matches, champion, (Sets 14–1, games 88–40).
1994, seeded No. 1, won 0 matches, lost Lori McNeil, 1st Round.
1995, seeded No. 1, won 7 matches, champion, (Sets 14–2, games 95–42).
1996, seeded No. 1, won 7 matches, champion, (Sets 14–1, games 88–45).
1997, did not play.
1998, seeded No. 4, won 2 matches, lost Natasha Zvereva, 3rd round.
1999, seeded No. 2, won 6 matches, lost Lindsay Davenport, final.

**Matches:** 74–7; sets 151–29; games 1048–530.

**Longest Match:** 1st round 1984, beat Susan Mascarin 6–4 5–7 10–8 -a total of 40 games.

**Age on first winning singles:** 19 years 18 days

**Age on last winning singles:** 27 years 22 days

**Overall Record:**

|  | Titles | Matches Played | Won | Lost |
|---|---|---|---|---|
| Singles | 7 | 81 | 74 | 7 |
| Doubles | 1 | 20 | 14 | 6 |
| Mixed | 0 | 9 | 7 | 2 |
| Total | 8 | 110 | 95 | 15 |

**Career Achievements:**

*The Championships, Wimbledon:* singles 1988, 1989, 1991, 1992, 1993, 1995, 1996; doubles, 1988.

*US Championships:* singles 1988, 1989, 1993, 1995, 1996.

*French Championships:* singles 1987, 1988, 1993, 1995, 1996, 1999.

*Australian Championships:* singles 1988, 1989, 1990, 1994.

*Total Grand Slam titles:* 23 – singles 22; doubles 1.

*Grand Slam Singles:* 1988.

*Italian Championships:* singles 1987.

*German Championships:* singles 1986, 1987, 1988, 1989, 1991, 1992, 1993, 1994; doubles 1986.

*WTA Tour Championships:* singles 1987, 1989, 1993, 1995, 1996.

*Olympic Games:* singles 1988 gold medal, 1992 silver medal.

*German Federation/Fed Cup team:* 1986, 1987, 1989, 1991–1993, 1996 winning 28 from 32 matches in 20 ties (singles 20–2; doubles 8–2).

*Won:* 107 singles titles, 11 doubles titles.

*Played:* 1017 singles matches, winning 902.

*Prize money:* $21,895,277.

**Full name:** Stefanie (Steffi) Maria Graf/Agassi
**Born:** 14th June, 1969, Neckarau, Mannheim, Germany.
**Married:** Andre Agassi on 22nd October 2001, Las Vegas, Nevada, USA.

# Conchita Martinez

## 1994

### The Reign of Spain

For those intelligent enough to read the tea leaves, the message were there, clear for all to see. For five years in a row Conchita Martinez had reached the quarter-finals of the French Open. No sur- prise there. Spanish women are expected to excel on clay. Then, in that fifth year, 1993, Conchita went on to Wimbledon and reached the semi-finals where she pressed defending champion Steffi Graf hard in the first set before going down 7–6 6–3. Now that WAS a bit of a surprise.

Clearly Conchita had been inspired by that performance but she must have realised, like everyone else, that Steffi, undefeated on grass for three years, was still the best player in the world. Enter Lori McNeil. At Wimbledon the following year the black American pulled off one of the greatest upsets in tennis history. On a dark and stormy afternoon worthy of a doom-laden Wagnerian opera, Lori beat the nervy champion 7–5 7–6 in a first round match of unbearable tension that was punctuated with rain breaks.

Now the field was wide open. Three at least of the proven grass court players fancied their chances of snatching the title. One of them, the 1991 finalist Gabriela Sabatini, had a fourth round meeting against the improving American Lindsay Davenport, aged 18, whose powerful game was potentially built for success on grass. The other two, Jana Novotna and Martina Navratilova, would meet one another in the quarter-finals. The 37–year-old nine-time champion was the last person to have beaten Steffi in a Wimbledon final and with the champion gone still harboured thoughts of a tenth singles crown.

In the first of those matches Davenport proved to have too much power from the baseline for Sabatini whose lack of penetration was her undoing. Navratilova was on song against Novotna and, despite losing the twelve game opening set, con- ceded only one more game as she swept through to the semi-finals.

Martinez took her chances well against a slightly hesitant Davenport to inflict a three sets defeat on the disappointed American. She then ended McNeil's charge in

a gripping semi-final that went down to the wire, 3–6 6–2 10–8. Thus, she was the first Spanish woman to reach the final since Lili de Alvarez in 1928.

Navratilova had no problems in her semi against Gigi Martinez, a doubles expert who looked lost on the singles court against the former champion.

What a final these two produced! Although she looked a mite slower than of yore Navratilova still exuded confidence as she attempted to impose herself at the net. Martinez, though, was not intimidated, perhaps because she remembered her three wins in Rome against the left-handed former champion since losing their first encounter there in 1990. If she could win on clay, why not on grass? As the match progressed the Martinez backhand, fizzing with topspin, began to find winning angles against the charging Navratilova. Occasionally at first, then more frequently, Martinez herself would flatten out some of her drives and charge in for a winning volley.

After losing the first set 4–6 Navratilova raced to 4–0 in the second and had soon taken the set 6–3 to level the match. At courtside Martina's coach Craig Kardon, plus Billie Jean King were urging her on along with Martina's parents on a rare visit to watch her play.

When Martina lost her serve with a double fault in the long opening game of the final set after leading 40–15 you sensed that the tide had turned for Martinez. The Spaniard looked increasingly confident as Martina's challenge faltered. After levelling at 2–2 Martina had one last chance. With Martinez a break ahead once more at 4–3, she fell behind 15–40 but recovered to hold for 5–3. It was virtually the end. Trailing 15–40 on her serve, Martina missed her backhand approach and it was all over. Conchita had made history. She had become the first Spanish woman to claim the Wimbledon title.

This was the pinnacle of Conchita's career. The year following her Wimbledon win she claimed six Tour titles and reached the semi-finals of all four Grand Slams – enough to propel her to No. 2 in the rankings at the year's end. A run to the finals of the Australian Open in 1998 was the closest she got to another major title but Martina Hingis ended that dream in straight sets.

For someone who had contributed to five Spanish Fed Cup successes and had won Olympic Silver and bronze in doubles with Artantxa Sanchez-Vicario it was fitting that the International Tennis Federation should have presented the two of them with the ITF's inaugural Award of Excellence in 2002.

**Wimbledon Singles Record:**
1992, seeded No.8, won 1 match, lost Natalia Zvereva, 2nd round.
1993, seeded No.6, won 5 matches, lost Steffi Graf, semi-final.
1994, seeded No.3, won 7 matches, champion, (sets 14–4, games 104–69).
1995, seeded No.3, won 5 matches, lost Arantxa Sanchez Vicario, semi-final.
1996, seeded No.3, won 3 matches, lost Kimiko Date, 4th round.
1997, seeded No.10, won 2 matches, lost Helena Sukova, 3rd round.

1998, seeded No.8, won 2 matches, lost Samantha Smith, 3rd round.
1999, unseeded, won 2 matches, lost Lisa Raymond, 3rd round.
2000, seeded No.4, won 1 match, lost to Sonya Jevaseelan, 2nd round.
2001, seeded No.19, won 4 matches, lost to Justine Henin, quarter-final.
2002, unseeded, won 2 matches, lost to Lisa Raymond, 3rd round.
2003, seeded No.18, won 2 matches, lost to Anastasia Myskina, 3rd round.
2004, seeded No.22, won 0 matches, lost to Milagros Sequera, 1st round.

**Matches:** 36–2; sets 77–32; games 590–408

**Longest match:** Semi-final in 1994, beat Lori McNeil 3–6 6–2 10–8 – a total of 35 games.

**Age on winning singles:** 22 years 77 days.

**Overall Record:**

|         | Titles | Matches Played | Won | Lost |
|---------|--------|--------|-----|------|
| Singles | 1      | 48     | 36  | 12   |
| Doubles | 0      | 29     | 17  | 12   |
| Mixed   | 0      | 0      | 0   | 0    |
| Total   | 1      | 77     | 53  | 24   |

**Career Achievements:**
*The Championships, Wimbledon:* singles 1994.
*Total Grand Slam titles:* 1 – singles 1.
*Italian Championships:* singles 1993–1996, doubles 2002.
*German Championships:* singles 1998, 2000, doubles 2000.
*Olympic Games:* doubles 1992, silver, doubles 1996, bronze, doubles 2004, silver
*Spanish Federation/Fed Cup team:* 1988–1996, 1998, 2000–2004 winning 68 from 91
    matches in 53 ties (singles 47–18, doubles 21–5).
*Won:* 32 singles titles, 11 doubles titles.
*Played:* 989 singles matches, winning 711.
*Prize money:* $11,009,539.

**Full name:** Inmaculada Concepcion (Conchita) Martinez
**Born:** 16th April, 1972, Monzon, nr. Huesca, Spain.

# Martina Hingis

## 1997

## *Infant Prodigy*

Never has there been a more precocious champion. When Martina Hingis teamed with Helena Sukova in 1996 to win the Wimbledon doubles title, the demure Swiss Miss had spent just 15 years and 282 days on planet Earth. Martina thus became the youngest ever winner of a Grand Slam title. Not even the legendary Lottie Dod, winner of the first of her five Wimbledon singles titles in 1887, aged 15 years 285 days, had achieved as much.

The following year, still only 16, Martina captured three of the four Grand Slam crowns (an unexpected loss to Iva Majoli in the French final prevented a Grand Slam). It seemed likely that the tactically aware youngster was about to rewrite all the record books.

Many records she did break but, like the great Maureen Connolly before her, Martina had her career cut short by a serious injury. When a damaged left ankle forced her to announce her retirement in October 2002 she could look back on 40 tournament successes in singles – five of them Grand Slams – and 36 doubles crowns, nine of them majors. After becoming the youngest-ever world No. 1 in March 1997 at 16 years 6 months, Martina would spend a total of 209 weeks at the top until 2002, a spell interrupted intermittently by Lindsay Davenport as the lead changed hands eight times. Furthermore, for 35 weeks Martina was ranked No. 1 simultaneously in singles and doubles, a feat achieved by only four other players.

Raised by her mother Melanie Molitor, herself a former Czech champion who named her daughter after Martina Navratilova, the youngster took to the tennis court like a duck to water. The eager toddler first held a racket aged two and a couple of years later was competing in a tournament for tinies. When Martina was eight Melanie left her husband Karol and moved with Martina to Trubbach in Switzerland. There she drilled her daughter on the practice court and taught her the importance of control and surprise.

The lessons were well learned. Blessed with a keen eye and split-second timing, even as a junior Martina was able to dictate the course of a rally by taking the ball early and using her control of the racket face to project the ball to unexpected

angles. Aged 12, and looking as if a strong gust of wind would blow her over, she embarrassed a series of older girls by winning the French Open junior title. A year later she was the 1994 Wimbledon junior champion with her opponents terrified of her ability to make them look stupid.

It was a quality that Martina carried over to the women's game as she entered the pro Tour at the end of that year. Many would be the players of experience who found themselves tied up in Swiss knots.

Following her Grand Slam triple in 1997 Martina retained her Australian title the following January at the expense of Conchita Martinez but then was brought down at the semi-final stage both in Paris and at Wimbledon. In New York she was beaten in the US Open final by Davenport. This last was an important victory because it proved to that group of power players (which included the Williams sisters, Capriati and Seles, as well as Davenport herself) that it was possible to hit Martina off the court as long as you did not make too many errors.

In five more major finals that is exactly what happened and the increasingly frustrated Martina began to realise that she did not have the equipment to win another major. In Paris 1999 Graf beat her after saving a match point and seeing her younger opponent dissolve into tears. Reacting badly to that defeat and parting company with her mother for the first time at a major Championship, Martina lost in the first round at Wimbledon to an inspired Jelena Dokic. In New York it was Serena who blasted through her defences.

Australia offered the last hope of salvation. Martina had been victorious there in three successive finals against Pierce, Martinez and Mauresmo respectively. When she arrived in the 2000 final to face Davenport, Martina was on an Australian winning streak of 27 matches. Unfortunately for her Lindsay remembered the winning formula from the US Open two years earlier and smote her way to another victory, 6–1 7–5.

There followed two more defeats in successive Australian finals, both at the hands Jennifer Capriati, the American who was marvellously restored as a force in the game after a spell in the wilderness. The first was an easy straight sets win but the second, in 2002, was a cruel affair. Leading 6–4 4–0 Hingis seemed to have the title once more in her grasp but the brutal heat, more than 30 degrees Celsius, seemed to sap Martina's strength. Four times she held Championship point. Four times Capriati responded brilliantly. Eventually it was the greater physical strength of Capriati that prevailed.

At that moment one sensed that Martina had been emotionally scarred. Clever and resourceful as she was – no woman has ever shown greater tactical awareness, none has counter-attacked with greater skill – Martina simply lacked the weight of shot, especially on serve, necessary to beat the power brokers. Deep within Martina must have feared that the game was up. She might never again rule the tennis roost as she had done so magnificently in a gentler age, albeit only five years earlier. The game had changed and Martina did not have the physical resources to change with it.

It was really no surprise when she decided to retire. For one who had been the best ever for her age, playing second best cannot have been any fun at all. But there were compensations. Aged just 22, at least there was time to think of ways to spend some of her tennis earnings – $18,344,660 from prize money alone and third highest of all time behind Graf and Navratilova. Released from the discipline of an athlete's relentless routine, there was also the delightful prospect of leading a normal life.

**Wimbledon Singles Record:**
1995, unseeded, won 0 matches, lost Steffi Graf, 1st round.
1996, seeded No.16, won 3 matches, lost Steffi Graf, 4th round.
1997, seeded No.1, won 7 matches, champion, (sets 14–1, games 86–42).
1998, seeded No.1, won 5 matches, lost Jana Novotna, semi-final.
1999, seeded No.1, won 0 matches, lost Jelena Dokic, 1st round.
2000, seeded No.1, won 4 matches, lost Venus Williams, quarter-final.
2001, seeded No.1, won 0 matches, lost Virginia Ruano Pascual, 1st round.

**Matches:** 19–6; sets 39–15; games 275–187

**Longest match:** Quarter-final in 2000, lost to Venus Williams 6–3 4–6 6–4 – a total of 29 games.

**Age on winning singles:** 16 years 278 days.

**Overall Record:**

|  | Titles | Matches | | |
| --- | --- | --- | --- | --- |
|  |  | Played | Won | Lost |
| Singles | 1 | 25 | 19 | 6 |
| Doubles | 2 | 20 | 17 | 3 |
| Mixed | 0 | 6 | 4 | 2 |
| Total | 3 | 51 | 40 | 11 |

**Career Achievements:**
*The Championships, Wimbledon:* singles 1997; doubles 1996, 1998.
*U.S. Championships:* singles 1997; doubles 1998.
*French Championships:* doubles 1998, 2000.
*Australian Championships:* singles 1997–1999; doubles 1997–1999, 2002.
*Total Grand Slam titles:* 14 – singles 5, doubles 9.
*Grand Slam doubles:* 1998. (Australian – Mirjana Lucic; French, Wimbledon, USA – Jana Novotna)
*Italian Championships:* singles 1998; doubles 1999.
*German Championships:* singles 1999.
*WTA Tour Championships:* singles 1998, 2000; doubles 1999, 2000.
*Swiss Fed Cup Team:* 1995–1998 winning 26 from 30 matches in 14 ties (singles 18–2, doubles 8–2).
*Won:* 40 singles titles, 36 doubles titles.
*Played:* 571 singles matches, winning 471.
*Prize money:* $18,344,660.

**Full name:** Martina Hingis
**Born:** 30th September, 1980, Kosice, Czecholslovakia.

# Jana Novotna

## 1998

## *Persistence Rewarded*

For Jana Novotna 13 is a lucky number. It was on her 13th visit to Wimbledon in 1998 that the shy and talented Czech at last won the title she had first threatened to win five years earlier.

On that occasion, cheered on by her coach Hana Mandlikova, Jana had built a 4–1 lead in the final set against defending champion Steffi Graf with some enterprising net play. Sadly she had choked on her lead and lost the match. The scenes of a tearful Jana being comforted by the Duchess of Kent in an emotional presentation ceremony on Centre Court were beamed around the world.

Against Nathalie Tauziat in the 1998 final the 29–year-old held her nerve superbly, as she had done one round earlier to revenge herself against the Swiss teenager Martina Hingis who had beaten her in the 1997 final. This time Jana could afford to smile as the Duchess presented her with the famous silver-gilt Venus Rosewater dish. Jana had just made herself the oldest first-time Wimbledon winner in the open era and for good measure she added the doubles title as well in partnership with Martina Hingis.

In fact it was in doubles that we had first come to admire Jana's volleying skills and smooth athleticism. During her 13 years on the Tour Jana won no fewer than 76 doubles titles, 12 of them Grand Slams with five different partners, plus four in mixed, all with America's Jim Pugh.

Twice Jana won three of the major ladies doubles crowns in the same year, in 1990 with Helena Sukova and in 1998 with Martina Hingis. On both occasions the pair were voted the WTA Doubles Team of the Year, an accolade Jana received on three other occasions.

When she retired in 1999 with 24 singles title to her name there was a feeling that Jana should have achieved more. The immense all-court talent was there for all to see but there was also the suggestion of mental frailty on important occasions, something she was usually able to overcome in doubles with the help of a partner but found more difficult in singles.

**Wimbledon Singles Record**:

1986, unseeded, won 0 matches, lost Sue Mascarin, 1st round.

1987, unseeded, won 3 matches, lost Steffi Graf, 4th round.

1988, unseeded, won 1 match, lost Helen Sukova, 2nd round.

1989, seeded No.10, won 3 matches, lost Laura Golarsa, 4th round.

1990, seeded No.13, won 4 matches, lost Steffi Graf, quarter-final.

1991, seeded No.6, won 1 match, lost Brenda Scultz, 2nd round.

1992, seeded No.11, won 2 matches, lost Patti Fendick, 3rd round.

1993, seeded No.8, won 6 matches, lost Steffi Graf, final.

1994, seeded No.5, won 4 matches, lost Martina Navratilova, quarter-final.
1995, seeded No.4, won 5 matches, lost Steffi Graf, semi-final.
1996, seeded No.6, won 4 matches, lost Steffi Graf, quarter-final.
1997, seeded No.3, won 6 matches, lost Martina Hingis, final.
1998, seeded No.3, won 7 matches, champion, (Sets 14–1, games 91–52).
1999, seeded No.5, won 4 matches, lost Lindsay Davenport, quarter-final.

**Matches:** 50–13 sets 107–38; games 793–537.

**Longest Match:** 4th round 1997, beat Mary Joe Fernandez 5–7 6–4 7–5 – a total of 34 games.

**Age on winning singles:** 29 years 275 days.

**Overall Record:**

| | Titles | Matches | | |
| --- | --- | --- | --- | --- |
| | | Played | Won | Lost |
| Singles | 1 | 63 | 50 | 13 |
| Doubles | 4 | 64 | 56 | 8 |
| Mixed | 1 | 17 | 14 | 3 |
| Total | 6 | 144 | 120 | 24 |

**Career Achievements:**
*The Championships, Wimbledon:* singles 1998; doubles, 1989, 1990, 1995, 1998; mixed 1989.
*U.S. Championships:* doubles 1994, 1997, 1998; mixed 1988.
*French Championships:* doubles 1990, 1991, 1998.
*Australian Championships:* doubles 1990, 1995; mixed 1988, 1989.
*Total Grand Slam titles:* 17 – singles 1; doubles 12; mixed 4.
*Italian Championships:* doubles 1988, 1993.
*German Championships:* doubles 1992, 1997.
*WTA Tour Championships:* singles 1997; doubles 1995, 1997.
*Olympic Games:* doubles 1988, silver, 1996, silver.
*Czechoslovakia/Czech Republic Federation/Fed Cup team:* 1987–1993, 1995–1998 winning 33 from 45 matches in 33 ties (singles 22–7, doubles 11–5).
*Won:* 24 singles titles, 76 doubles titles.
*Played:* 791 singles matches, winning 568.
*Prize money:* $11,249,134.

**Full name:** Jana Novotna.
**Born:** 2nd October, 1968, Brno, Czechoslovakia

# Lindsay Davenport

## 1999

### Californian Clout

She may have been voted the most friendly and co-operative player on the Tour by journalists at the 2000 French Open but, on court, Lindsay Davenport is a mean match-winning machine, a tigress who prowls the baseline ready to pounce.

One of the tallest players in women's tennis, Lindsay uses her 6' 2" and her long reach to pound those hammer blows on forehand and double-handed backhand that have brought her 45 singles titles and 35 in doubles during her 11 years on the Tour and

earned her over $18 million dollars from prize money alone by the end of 2004. Her powerful game has also contributed to three US Fed Cup victories in 1996, 1999 and 2000.

If you asked Lindsay which of those successes has given her most pleasure she would probably pick her 1996 Olympic gold medal in Atlanta ahead of her 1998 US Open, her 1999 Wimbledon, her 2000 Australian crown or any of her three Grand Slam doubles titles.

Why? First because her dad, Wink, was an Olympian in his youth as a member of the US Volleyball team and also because it was in Atlanta that Lindsay made a mental breakthrough when her captain Billie Jean King convinced her that, with the right preparation, she could one day rule the world of tennis.

Until that moment Lindsay had found it difficult to find the right training routine to get herself in proper shape. At times her lack of mobility produced a look of despondency as she lost to players she knew she should be beating.

Eventually, though, Lindsay did apply herself properly with the help of Robert Van't Hof who spent seven years altogether with her on the road as she worked to achieve her potential. The goal was reached in October 1998 when Lindsay fulfilled Billie Jean's expectations by achieving the No. 1 world ranking for the first time. She reached that pinnacle after beating defending champion and world No. 1 Martina Hingis in the US Open final to earn a first Grand Slam singles title. This victory, on her mother's birthday, was an emotional moment.

Equally emotional was the Wimbledon win over seven-times champion Graf in 1999 and the following year's defeat of Martina Hingis in the Australian Open final that ended the Swiss prodigy's 27 match-winning streak in Melbourne. Lindsay had now firmly established herself as a member of the game's elite.

When Van't Hof and Lindsay parted company amicably at the end of 2001 she joined forces for a while with doubles expert Rick Leach, the brother of her husband Jon whom she married in April 2003. Since that time she has been guided by Adam Peterson.

All Lindsay's coaches would attest to her friendly demeanour and high work rate. One of the most popular players among her peers, it is no surprise that they have elected Lindsay several times to represent them on the Players Council.

Lindsay's career is still a work in progress and her chief concern as she heads towards her 30s will be to stay clear of injury. Like so many of her fellow pros, Lindsay has had her share of problems. A left wrist injury in 1999 was the first to afflict her. In 2000 it was an injured back. The following year a knee injury kept her off court for 2½ months and surgery was required in 2002 to fix the problem necessitating more time away from competition. In 2003 it was a severe foot condition that affected her performances and kept her inactive again as surgery was performed in October. Mercifully 2004 was relatively stress free though there were minor interruptions. A shoulder strain during a successful Hopman Cup campaign in January forced her to miss Sydney but did not prevent her from reaching the last eight at the Australian Open. A knee problem flared again in Paris and tendinitis in her right wrist caused her to miss New Haven in August.

Nevertheless, Lindsay won seven tournaments in 2004, more than any of her peers, and ended the year atop the rankings once more. The tigress was snarling again.

## Wimbledon Singles Record:

1993, unseeded, won 2 matches, lost Nathalie Tauziat, 3rd round.
1994, seeded No.9, won 4 matches, lost Conchita Martinez, quarter-final.
1995, seeded No.7, won 3 matches, lost Mary Joe Fernandez, 4th round.
1996, seeded No.8, won 1 match, lost Larisa Neiland, 2nd round.
1997, seeded No.5, won 1 match, lost Denisa Chladkova, 2nd round.
1998, seeded No.2, won 4 matches, lost Nathalie Tauziat, quarter-final.
1999, seeded No.3, won 7 matches, champion, (sets 14–0, games 86–37).
2000, seeded No.2, won 6 matches, lost Venus Williams, final.
2001, seeded No.3, won 5 matches, lost Venus Williams, semi-final.
2002, did not play
2003, seeded No.5, won 4 matches, lost Venus Williams, quarter-final.
2004, seeded No.5, won 5 matches, lost Maria Sharapova, semi-final.

**Matches:** 42–10; sets 88–28; games 622–401

**Longest Match:** – three times – 30 games.

**Age on winning singles:** 23 years 26 days.

**Overall Record:**

| | Titles | Matches Played | Won | Lost |
|---|---|---|---|---|
| Singles | 1 | 52 | 42 | 10 |
| Doubles | 1 | 30 | 24 | 6 |
| Mixed | 0 | 30 | 23 | 7 |
| Total | 2 | 112 | 89 | 23 |

**Career Achievements:**

*The Championships, Wimbledon:* singles 1999; doubles 1999
*U.S. Championships:* singles 1998; doubles 1997
*French Championships:* doubles 1996
*Australian Championships:* singles 2000
*Total Grand Slam titles:* 6 – singles 3, doubles 3
*German Championships:* doubles, 1997, 1998
*WTA Tour Championships:* singles 1999, doubles 1996, 1998
*Olympic Games:* singles 1996 gold
*U.S. Federation/Fed Cup team:* 1993–2000, 2002 winning 28 from 30 matches in 18 ties (singles 23–2, doubles 5–0)
*Won:* 45 singles titles, 35 doubles titles.
*Played:* 805 matches winning 635.
*Prize money:* $18,694,975.

**Full name:** Lindsay Ann Davenport/Leach
**Born:** 8th June, 1976, Palos Verdes, California, USA.
**Married:** Jonathan Leach, 25th April 2003, Kona, Hawaii, USA.

# Venus Williams

## 2000, 2001

### Power Personified

It was apparent the first time we saw her at Wimbledon in 1997 that Venus Williams had the potential to become a champion. Tall, athletic and powerful the young American, just 17, lost that year in the first round to Magdalena Grzbowska of Poland as she came to terms with a new surface. However, Venus did enough that day in winning the first set to suggest that it would only be a matter of time before she fulfilled the prophesy of her father.

The story of Richard Williams and his tennis daughters reads more like a novel than an episode from real life with a plot so preposterous that any sane publisher receiving the manuscript would have tossed it straight into the waste paper basket.

Consider the facts. An African-American, living in a tough part of Los Angeles, is watching on television the final of a women's Tour event and hears the commentator say that one of the players has already won more than $1 million in prize money.

Despite having had no coaching experience, this ambitious man decides he will coach one of his three daughters to stardom. He purchases books and videos on coaching and gets to work. Unfortunately none of his daughters appears to have the aptitude for tennis. Obviously he needs new material. Accordingly he hides his wife's contraceptive pills and hopes that she will produce another daughter for him. In fact she produces two – Venus and Serena, born 15 months apart.

From the first Richard has one objective – to turn his new young daughters into tennis champions. Life is hard. Gang warfare pervades this corner of the world and violence is a way of life. The girls keep their eyes about them as they accompany their mother Oracene, a devout Jehova's Witness, on her door-to-door visits. Even trips to the tennis courts in the local park are hazardous. Their journey is often punctuated with the sound of gunshots. Before Richard can start his tennis lessons they have to sweep broken glass from the courts. Richard demands absolute commitment. He drills the girls mercilessly, all the time telling them that they will one day become champions. The girls improve. To confirm that he is on the right lines Richard visits long-time coach Rick Macci who gives him reassurance and encouragement. When she is twelve Venus is allowed to enter a few junior tournaments. She never loses and has several wins over older girls in compiling a 63–0 match record. Serena simply continues to work away in private.

Stories circulate in the tennis world about this crazy American father who claims that his two daughters will soon become world-beaters. Obviously this is a preposterous idea. Whoever heard of a young player by-passing junior tennis and expecting to succeed? How could they possibly become match tough without competing?

The answers are not long in coming. In 1994, aged just 14, Venus is launched on an unsuspecting world as a wild card entry at the WTA Tour tournament in Oakland. In her first match Venus beats an experienced pro, Shaun Stafford, 6–3 6–4 and leads world No. 2, Arantxa Sanchez-Vicario, 6–2 3–1 before being overhauled.

After playing just three tournaments in 1995 and five in 1996, Venus entered the 1997 season much stronger physically. Her powerful forehands and double-handed backhands looked as if they would kill anything in their path. After reaching the quarter-finals at three Tour events she smote her way to the final of her first US Open after saving match points in a tough semi-final against Irina Spirlea. Another young prodigy, Martina Hingis, three months younger than Venus but already the world No. 1, beat her in straight sets.

There follow two years of consolidation – plus some frustration – as sister Serena beat her to a first Grand Slam title at the 1999 US Open. Venus sat stony-faced watching that match with her mother Oracene, but the experience might have been the catalyst for what happened in 2000.

Despite missing the first four months of the season with a wrist injury, Venus plundered the silverware at Wimbledon. A difficult semi-finals win over Serena was followed by a straight sets win over fellow American Lindsay Davenport. Not since Althea Gibson, the 1957 and '58 champion, had an Afro-American woman won at Wimbledon. The sheer pace and power displayed by both Williams and Davenport that day underlined the change that had come over the game. Power now ruled over finesse. The days of Hingis were numbered.

Two months later Venus beat Davenport again to capture her first US Open title and capped a tremendous year by taking the gold medal in singles and doubles, with Serena, at the Sydney Olympics.

A year later she had retained her two Grand Slam titles titles. Justine Henin was her victim at Wimbledon, sister Serena at the US Open. This was the first Grand Slam final between sisters since Maud Watson beat Lillian Watson at the first Wimbledon for women in 1884. Another triumph for the sisters had come in January that year when the capture of the Australian Open doubles title completed a career doubles Grand Slam.

Despite appearing in five Grand Slam finals since, three of them in 2002 and two the following year, Venus has not won another Grand Slam crown. A series of injuries plus a growing interest in interior design have inhibited progress on court. It remains to be seen whether she can recapture the glorious form of 2002 when, just as Richard had predicted, Serena was the No. 1 player in the world and Venus No. 2.

## Wimbledon Singles Record:

1997, unseeded won 0 matches, lost Magdalena Grzybowska, 1st round.
1998, seeded No.7, won 4 matches, lost Jana Novotna, quarter-final.
1999, seeded No.6, won 4 matches, lost Steffi Graf, quarter-final.
2000, seeded No.5, won 7 matches, champion, (sets 14–1, games 91–53)
2001, seeded No.2, won 7 matches, champion, (sets 14–2, games 94–39)
2002, seeded No.1, won 6 matches, lost Serena Williams, final.
2003, seeded No.4, won 6 matches, lost Serena Williams, final.
2004, seeded No.3, won 1 match, lost Karolina Sprem, 2nd round.

**Matches:** 35–6; sets 73–19; games 520–290

**Longest Match:** Quarter-final in 2000, beat Martina Hingis 6–3 4–6 6–4 – a total of 29 games.

**Age on winning singles:** 20 years, 21 days.

**Age on last winning singles:** 21 years, 21 days.

**Overall Record:**

|         | Titles | Matches Played | Won | Lost |
|---------|--------|--------|-----|------|
| Singles | 2      | 41     | 35  | 6    |
| Doubles | 2      | 17     | 16  | 1    |
| Mixed   | 0      | 9      | 6   | 3    |
| Total   | 4      | 67     | 57  | 10   |

## Career Achievements:

*The Championships, Wimbledon:* singles 2000, 2001; doubles 2000, 2002
*U.S. Championships:* singles 2000, 2001; doubles 1999
*French Championships:* doubles 1999
*Australian Championships:* doubles 2001, 2003; mixed 1998
*Total Grand Slam titles:* 11 – singles 4, doubles 7
*Italian Championships:* singles 1999
*Olympic Games:* singles 2000 gold, doubles 2000 gold
*U.S. Fed Cup team:* 1999, 2003, 2004, winning 10 from 11 matches in 4 ties (singles 7–1, doubles 3–0)
*Won:* 31 singles titles, 9 doubles titles.
*Played:* 459 singles, winning 375.
*Prize money:* $14,503,591.

**Full name:** Venus Ebone Starr Williams
**Born:** 17th June, 1980, Lynwood, California, U.S.A.

# Serena Williams

## 2002, 2003

### *Sister Superior*

Like her sister, Venus, Serena Williams was the subject of a wild gamble by her father Richard to raise tennis champions. Against all the odds, the gamble succeeded. Just as Richard had predicted, by the end of 2002, Serena and Venus were the Nos. 1 and 2 ranked players in the world. By any measure, it was an astonishing achievement.

Serena's success was the more remarkable because, unlike her sister, she did not have a competitive junior career of any sort. In 1995, aged just 14, Serena was given a wild card into the qualifying event in Quebec, largely on the strength of her sister's extraordinary debut at the same age. Serena was beaten comprehensively in her first match by a little-known American, Annie Miller. Richard realised she was not ready and wisely kept her out of competition for a full year.

Serena's return in 1997 was spectacular. In only her second main draw in Chicago, a wild card ranked 304, she beat world No. 7 Mary Pierce and No. 4 Monica Seles before losing in the semi-finals to Lindsay Davenport. The gauntlet had been thrown down. No player ranked as low had beaten two top-ten players in the same tournament before.

A first top 20 finish in 1998 included revenge against Davenport in Sydney and four more wins against players in the top ten in her fist 16 Tour matches, a record that still stands. It also included mixed doubles success with the tall Belarussian, Max Mirnyi, at Wimbledon and the US Open. There would also be ladies' doubles victories with sister Venus – two at the Australian Open, two at Wimbledon and one each at the French and US Opens, as well as an Olympic gold medal in Sydney.

Slightly shorter and more muscular than her sister, Serena's power from the back of the court drew gasps of astonishment from spectators and shudders from her opponents. Already her serve was considered the best ever seen on the women's Tour and her court coverage was equally impressive. If she ever learned to control her power it was clear she would sweep away any opposition....except, perhaps, her sister.

In 1999 it happened. Serena literally blasted her way to the final in Miami with victories over former world No. 1 Seles, the current No. 9 Amanda Coetzer and the reigning No. 1 Martina Hingis. In the final, the first on the main Tour between two sisters, Venus halted Serena's 16–match winning streak in three sets.

No-one, though, could halt Serena at the US Open. After cruising to the quarter-finals, first Seles then Davenport and Hingis were brushed aside as Serena, seeded 7, claimed her first Grand Slam crown, the lowest seed to win there and the first African-American winner since Althea Gibson in 1958. Serena was in the middle of a second 16–match winning streak which included victory in the Grand Slam Cup in Munich. In that final Serena scored her first ever win over Venus. This was a huge psychological barrier to overcome.

Clearly, though, the violence of her very physical game was having an adverse effect on Serena's body. Earlier in 1999 she had withdrawn from tournaments with patella tendinitis in her right knee and an injury to her right elbow. A bout of 'flu also forced her to miss Wimbledon.

In 2000 further injuries to knees and foot interrupted her season again. When she arrived at Wimbledon she had been away from the court since April and her loss to Venus in the semi-finals was a strange match full of hidden pressures that seemed to affect both players.

Nor could Serena recapture her form in 2001 as she continued to be dogged by injuries. Quarter-final finishes in Melbourne, Paris and at Wimbledon did not bode well for her chances at Flushing Meadows. Yet she did beat Justine Henin, Davenport and Hingis to reach the final where once again Venus was there to thwart her progress. It was the first Grand Slam final between sisters since the first Wimbledon for women in 1884 when Maud Watson had beaten her sister Lillian.

Despite missing the 2002 Australian Open (she had twisted her ankle in Sydney) Serena embarked on her most successful year to date. She won eight of the eleven tournaments she contested and swept the remaining three Grand Slams, beating Venus in all three finals.

Victory in the Australian Open of 2003 meant that Serena now held all four Grand Slams, a rare feat achieved by only four other women – Maureen Connolly, Margaret Court, Martina Navratilova and Steffi Graf. It seemed likely that Serena, like Connolly, Court and Graf, would go on to achieve a true Grand Slam as winner of the four major titles in the same year. That dream was ended in the Paris semi-final where Henin won a controversial match that ended Serena's Grand Slam streak at 33 matches. There were ugly scenes from the crowd that day when they booed Serena after a complaint about a line call. Henin, though, was thought by some to be guilty of gamesmanship when she said she was not ready to receive a winning Williams serve. It was all rather unedifying.

After successfully defending her Wimbledon crown Serena was again afflicted with injury. An operation on her left quadriceps on 1st August effectively ended her season and she was overtaken in the rankings by the two bright young Belgians, Henin and Kim Clijsters.

The year 2004 was equally disappointing. After winning her opening tournament in Miami Serena lost in the French quarter-finals to Capriati, lost her Wimbledon title to an inspired Maria Sharapova, lost to Davenport in the Los Angeles final, missed the US Open with injury and was beaten by Sharapova again in the final of the season ending WTA Tour Championships.

With growing outside commitments as actress and clothing designer it seems doubtful whether Serena would have the enthusiasm or the physical robustness to regain the heights of 2002 and 2003.

**Wimbledon Singles Record:**
1998, unseeded, won 2 matches, lost Virginia Ruano Pascual, 3rd round.
1999, did not play.
2000, seeded No.8, won 5 matches, lost Venus Williams, semi-final.
2001, seeded No.5, won 4 matches, lost Jennifer Capriati, quarter-final.
2002, seeded No.2, won 7 matches, champion, (sets 14–0, games 87–43).
2003, seeded No.1, won 7 matches, champion, (sets 14–2, games 90–50).
2004, seeded No.1, won 6 matches, lost Maria Sharapova, final.

**Matches:** 31–4; sets 63–11; games 422–215.

**Longest match:** Semi-final 2004, beat Amelie Mauresmo 6–7 7–5 6–4 – a total of 35 games.

**Age on winning singles:** 20 years 283 days

**Age on last winning singles:** 21 years 282 days

**Overall Record:**

|  | Titles | *Matches* Played | Won | Lost |
|---|---|---|---|---|
| Singles | 2 | 35 | 31 | 4 |
| Doubles | 2 | 17 | 16 | 1 |
| Mixed | 1 | 6 | 6 | 0 |
| Total | 5 | 58 | 53 | 5 |

**Career Achievements:**
*The Championships, Wimbledon:* singles 2002, 2003; doubles 2000, 2002; mixed 1998
*U.S. Championships:* singles 1999, 2002; doubles 1999; mixed 1998
*French Championships:* singles 2002; doubles 1999
*Australian Championships:* singles 2003; doubles 2001, 2003
*WTA Tour Championships:* singles 2001
*Total Grand Slam titles:* 14 – singles 6, doubles 8
*Italian Championships:* singles 2002
*Olympic Games:* doubles 2000 gold
*U.S. Fed Cup team:* 1999, 2003 winning 6 from 6 matches in 3 ties (singles 3–0, doubles 3–0)
*Won:* 25 singles titles, 11 doubles titles.
*Played:* 343 singles, winning 287.
*Prize money:* $14,798,661.

**Full name:** Serena Jamika Williams
**Born:** 26th September, 1981, Saginaw, Michigan, USA.

# Maria Sharapova

## 2004

### Russian Revelation

At first sight, the sudden success of the teenage Russian Maria Sharapova at Wimbledon in 2004 was a spectacular rags to riches story, but when you delve into her origins you understand the sacrifices Maria and her family had made to help her achieve her childhood dream.

Born within the deadly shadow of Chernobyl, Maria, like so many unfortunate victims, might have ended her days prematurely. But her father, Yuri, decided to move his young family away from Siberia to escape the potential danger of radiation.

When Maria was seven she was spotted at a tennis clinic in Moscow by Martina Navratilova who urged Yuri to take his daughter to the United States to develop her tennis. Two years later Yuri borrowed $700 from friends and flew with Maria to Florida leaving his wife Yelena behind for lack of funds.

After landing at Miami Airport one day in 1996 father and daughter made their way to Bradenton on the West coast of Florida. Penniless but hopeful, they arrived unannounced at Nick Bollettieri's famous Tennis Academy where Yuri pleaded to be allowed to display his daughter's talents.

It was a gamble which might have failed but as soon as Nick had seen the youngster hit a tennis ball he knew she had potential. There followed five arduous years of hard work. The first two, without her mother, were particularly tough for Maria who shared a dormitory with older girls while her father attempted to scratch a living as he learned to speak English. Yet she thrived in the competitive atmosphere at Bradenton and developed a work ethic that would eventually produce a tournament-hard competitor of the highest class.

Tall, blonde and beautiful, Maria's striking good looks have earned inevitable comparisons with another young Russian, Anna Kournikova. Like Anna, Maria has embarked on a modelling career, alongside her tennis, but that is where the comparison ends. Maria's modelling activities are few and remain secondary to her avowed ambition to become the best tennis player in the world.

Following Maria's sensational victory over defending champion Serena Williams in the 2004 Wimbledon final – a superb example of sustained aggression and deep concentration – there was a period of intense media hype. Trapped in the spotlight of international fame as the first ever Russian winner at Wimbledon, the new young champion found it difficult to sustain her high form and experienced a few unexpected losses. After all, Maria had been the lowest seed at 13 ever to win at Wimbledon. Furthermore, at 17 years and 25 days, she had been the third youngest singles champion in Wimbledon's history.

Yet by the season's end Maria had regained her composure and her confidence. As she swept to victory in the WTA Championships in Los Angeles it was clear that Maria Sharapova had the potential to become one of the game's great champions.

**Wimbledon Singles Record:**
2003, unseeded, won 3 matches, lost Svetlana Kuznetsova, 4th round.
2004, seeded No.13, won 7 matches, champion, (sets 14–2, games 94–51).

**Matches:** 10–1; sets 21–4; games 142–81.

**Longest Match:** Quarter-final in 2004, beat Ai Sugiyama 5–7 7–5 6–1 – a total of 31 games.

**Age on winning singles:** 17 years 25 days

**Overall Record:**

|  | Titles | Matches | | |
|---|---|---|---|---|
|  |  | Played | Won | Lost |
| Singles | 1 | 11 | 10 | 1 |
| Doubles | 0 | 0 | 0 | 0 |
| Mixed | 0 | 0 | 0 | 0 |
| Total | 1 | 11 | 10 | 1 |

**Career Achievements:**
*The Championships, Wimbledon:* singles 2004
*WTA Tour Championships:* singles 2004
*Won:* 7 singles titles, 3 doubles titles.
*Played:* 155 singles matches, winning 121.
*Prize money:* $2,752,068.

**Full name:** Maria Sharapova
**Born:** 17th April, 1987, Nyagan, USSR.

# Ladies' Singles Finals

## 1884–2004

From 1886 to 1921 the holder of the Ladies' Singles Championship did not compete until the Challenge Round, when she met the winner of the All Comers' Singles to decide The Championship. When the holder did not defend her title the winner of the All Comers' Singles automatically became Champion and the years this occurred are indicated by an asterisk.

1884 Maud Watson bt Lilian Watson 6–8 6–3 6–3
1885 Maud Watson bt Blanche Bingley 6–1 7–5
1886 Blanche Bingley bt Maud Watson 6–3 6–3
1887 Lottie Dod bt Blanche Bingley 6–2 6–0
1888 Lottie Dod bt Blanche Hillyard 6–3 6–3
*1889 Blanche Hillyard bt Lena Rice 4–6 8–6 6–4
*1890 Lena Rice bt M. Jacks 6–4 6–1
*1891 Lottie Dod bt Blanche Hillyard 6– 2 6–1
1892 Lottie Dod bt Blanche Hillyard 6–1 6–1
1893 Lottie Dod bt Blanche Hillyard 6–8 6–1 6–4
*1894 Blanche Hillyard bt Edith Austin 6–1 6–1
*1895 Charlotte Cooper bt Helen Jackson 7–5 8–6
1896 Charlotte Cooper bt Alice Pickering 6–2 6–3
1897 Blanche Hillyard bt Charlotte Cooper 5–7 7–5 6–2
*1898 Charlotte Cooper bt Louise Martin 6–4 6–4
1899 Blanche Hillyard bt Charlotte Cooper 6–2 6–3
1900 Blanche Hillyard bt Charlotte Cooper 4–6 6–4 6–4
1901 Charlotte Sterry bt Blanche Hillyard 6–2 6–2
1902 Muriel Robb bt Charlotte Sterry (4–6 13–11) 7–5 6–1
*1903 Dorothea Douglass bt Ethel Thomson 4–6 6–4 6–2
1904 Dorothea Douglass bt Charlotte Sterry 6–0 6–3
1905 May Sutton bt Dorothea Douglass 6–3 6–4
1906 Dorothea Douglass bt May Sutton 6–3 9–7
1907 May Sutton bt Dorothea Chambers 6–1 6–4
*1908 Charlotte Sterry bt Agatha Morton 6–4 6–4
*1909 Dora Boothby bt Agatha Morton 6–4 4–6 8–6
1910 Dorothea Chambers bt Dora Boothby 6–2 6–2
1911 Dorothea Chambers bt Dora Boothby 6–0 6–0
*1912 Ethel Larcombe bt Charlotte Sterry 6–3 6–1

\*1913 Dorothea Chambers bt Winifred McNair 6–0 6–4
1914 Dorothea Chambers bt Ethel Larcombe 7–5 6–4
1919 Suzanne Lenglen bt Dorothea Chambers 10–8 4–6 9–7
1920 Suzanne Lenglen bt Dorothea Chambers 6–3 6–0
1921 Suzanne Lenglen bt Elizabeth Ryan 6–2 6–0
1922 Suzanne Lenglen bt Molla Mallory 6–2 6–0
1923 Suzanne Lenglen bt Kathleen McKane 6–2 6–2
1924 Kathleen McKane bt Helen Wills 4–6 6–4 6–4
1925 Suzanne Lenglen bt Joan Fry 6–2 6–0
1926 Kathleen Godfree bt Lili de Alvarez 6–2 4–6 6–3
1927 Helen Wills bt Lili de Alvarez 6–2 6–4
1928 Helen Wills bt Lili de Alvarez 6–2 6–3
1929 Helen Wills bt Helen Jacobs 6–1 6–2
1930 Helen Moody bt Elizabeth Ryan 6–2 6–2
1931 Cilly Aussem bt Hilde Krahwinkel 6–2 7–5
1932 Helen Moody bt Helen Jacobs 6–3 6–1
1933 Helen Moody bt Dorothy Round 6–4 6–8 6–3
1934 Dorothy Round bt Helen Jacobs 6–2 5–7 6–3
1935 Helen Moody bt Helen Jacobs 6–3 3–6 7–5
1936 Helen Jacobs bt Hilde Sperling 6–2 4–6 7–5
1937 Dorothy Round bt Jadwiga Jedrzejowska 6–2 2–6 7–5
1938 Helen Moody bt Helen Jacobs 6–4 6–0
1939 Alice Marble bt Kay Stammers 6–2 6–0
1946 Pauline Betz bt Louise Brough 6–2 6–4
1947 Margaret Osborne bt Doris Hart 6–2 6–4
1948 Louise Brough bt Doris Hart 6–3 8–6
1949 Louise Brough bt Margaret du Pont 10–8 1–6 10–8
1950 Louise Brough bt Margaret du Pont 6–1 3–6 6–1
1951 Doris Hart bt Shirley Fry 6–1 6–0
1952 Maureen Connolly bt Louise Brough 7–5 6–3
1953 Maureen Connolly bt Doris Hart 8–6 7–5
1954 Maureen Connolly bt Louise Brough 6–2 7–5
1955 Louise Brough bt Beverley Fleitz 7–5 8–6
1956 Shirley Fry bt Angela Buxton 6–3 6–1
1957 Althea Gibson bt Darlene Hard 6–3 6–2
1958 Althea Gibson bt Angela Mortimer 8–6 6–2
1959 Maria Bueno bt Darlene Hard 6–4 6–3
1960 Maria Bueno bt Sandra Reynolds 8–6 6–0
1961 Angela Mortimer bt Christine Truman 4–6 6–4 7–5
1962 Karen Susman bt Vera Sukova 6–4 6–4
1963 Margaret Smith bt Billie Jean Moffit 6–3 6–4

1964 Maria Bueno bt Margaret Smith 6–4 7–9 6–3
1965 Margaret Smith bt Maria Bueno 6–4 7–5
1966 Billie Jean King bt Maria Bueno 6–3 3–6 6–1
1967 Billie Jean King bt Ann Jones 6–3 6–4
1968 Billie Jean King bt Judy Tegart 9–7 7–5
1969 Ann Jones bt Billie Jean King 3–6 6–3 6–2
1970 Margaret Court bt Billie Jean King 14–12 11–9
1971 Evonne Goolagong bt Margaret Court 6–4 6–1
1972 Billie Jean King bt Evonne Goolagong 6–3 6–3
1973 Billie Jean King bt Chris Evert 6–0 7–5
1974 Chris Evert bt Olga Morozova 6–0 6–4
1975 Billie Jean King bt Evonne Cawley 6–0 6–1
1976 Chris Evert bt Evonne Cawley 6–3 4–6 8–6
1977 Virginia Wade bt Betty Stove 4–6 6–3 6–1
1978 Martina Navratilova bt Chris Evert 2–6 6–4 7–5
1979 Martina Navratilova bt Chris Lloyd 6–4 6–4
1980 Evonne Cawley bt Chris Lloyd 6–1 7–6 (7–4)
1981 Chris Lloyd bt Hana Mandlikova 6–2 6–2
1982 Martina Navratilova bt Chris Lloyd 6–1 3–6 6–2
1983 Martina Navratilova bt Andrea Jaeger 6–0 6–3
1984 Martina Navratilova bt Chris Lloyd 7–6(7–5) 6–2
1985 Martina Navratilova bt Chris Lloyd 4–6 6–3 6–2
1986 Martina Navratilova bt Hana Mandlikova 7–6(7–1) 6–3
1987 Martina Navratilova bt Steffi Graf 7–5 6–3
1988 Steffi Graf bt Martina Navratilova 5–7 6–2 6–1
1989 Steffi Graf bt Martina Navratilova 6–2 6–7(1–7) 6–1
1990 Martina Navratilova bt Zina Garrison 6–4 6–1
1991 Steffi Graf bt Gabriela Sabatini 6–4 3–6 8–6
1992 Steffi Graf bt Monica Seles 6–2 6–1
1993 Steffi Graf bt Jana Novotna 7–6(8–6) 1–6 6–4
1994 Conchita Martinez bt Martina Navratilova 6–4 3–6 6–3
1995 Steffi Graf bt Arantxa Sanchez Vicario 4–6 6–1 7–5
1996 Steffi Graf bt Arantxa Sanchez Vicario 6–3 7–5
1997 Martina Hingis bt Jana Novotna 2–6 6–3 6–3
1998 Jana Novotna bt Nathalie Tauziat 6–4 7–6(7–2)
1999 Lindsay Davenport bt Steffi Graf 6–4 7–5
2000 Venus Williams bt Lindsay Davenport 6–3 7–6(7–3)
2001 Venus Williams bt Justine Henin 6–1 3–6 6–0
2002 Serena Williams bt Venus Williams 7–6(7–4) 6–3
2003 Serena Williams bt Venus Williams 4–6 6–4 6–2
2004 Maria Sharapova bt Serena Williams 6–1 6–4

# Index of Champions